THOMAS CUBBIN,
MASTER MARINER
and
THE WRECK OF THE *SERICA*

IN MEMORY OF

THOMAS

AGED 11 YEARS AND 3 MONTHS, AND

JAMES

1 YEAR AND 10 MONTHS, SONS OF THOMAS AND
MARY CUBBIN, THEY WERE DROWN'D IN EACH OTHERS
ARMS, IN THE SURF ON THE COAST OF MADAGASCAR, ON
THE 26TH MARCH 1868, AFTER ENDURING VERY GREAT
PRIVATION AND SUFFERINGS 11 DAYS IN A SMALL OPEN
BOAT, THROUGH THE FOUNDERING OF THE SHIP SERICA,
AFTER AN AWFUL HURRICANE IN THE INDIAN SEA.

*" TEACH ME TO LIVE THAT I MAY DREAD
THE GRAVE AS LITTLE AS MY BED."*

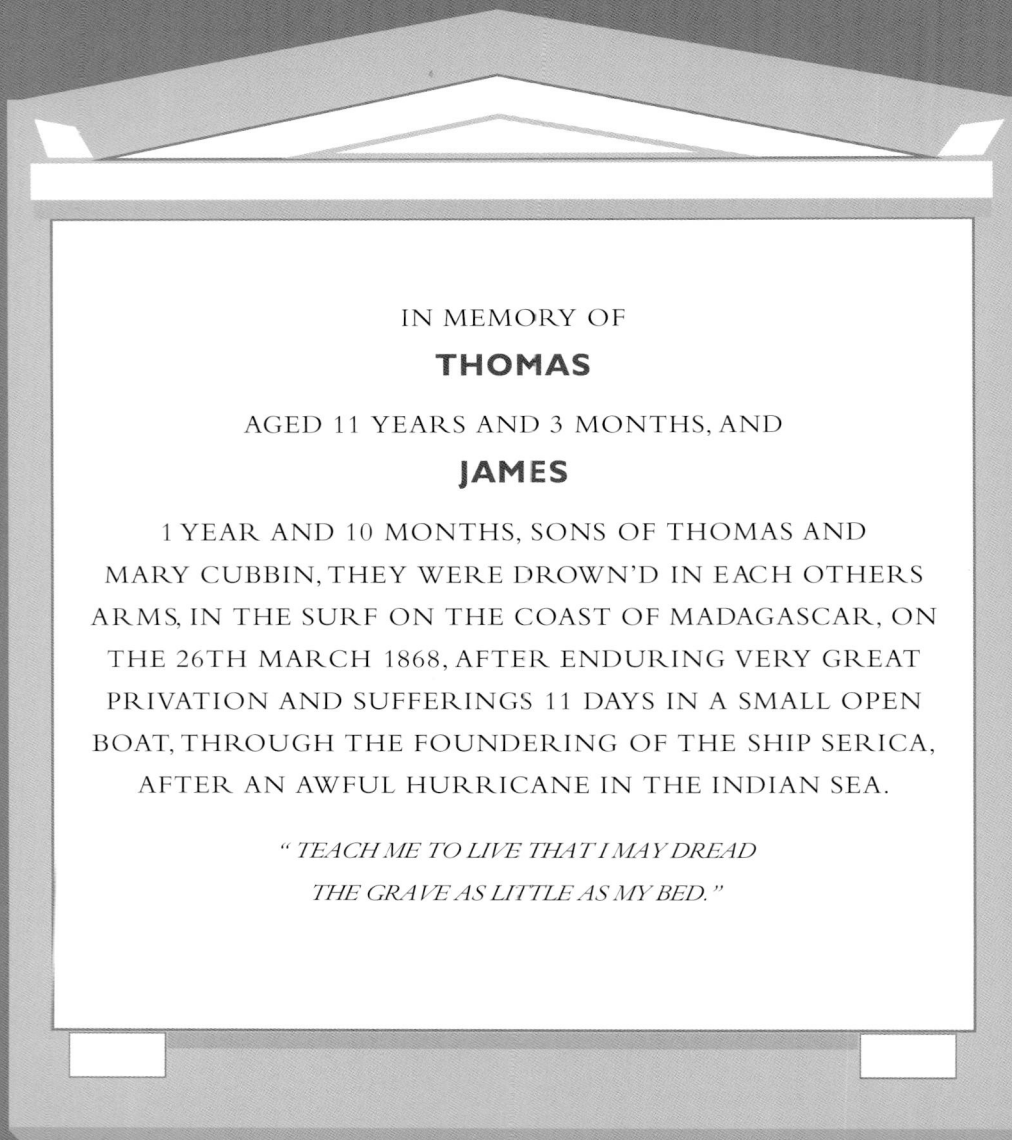

Memorial tablet on the south wall of Old Kirk Braddan.

'... I found a grave at the hands of strangers, and for ever do I wretchedly hear roaring even among the dead the hated thunder of the sea'.

'A Restless Grave', Aulus Licinius Archias (trans. J.W. Mackail)

Thomas Cubbin | Master Mariner

and the Wreck of the Serica

Cubbin's own account of the 1868 tragedy, with an historical Foreword

by Valerie Cottle

Manx Heritage Foundation

First published by the Manx Heritage Foundation 2011
PO Box 1986, Douglas, Isle of Man IM99 1SR
www.manxheritage.org

COVER DESIGN BY RUTH SUTHERLAND,
BASED ON A PAINTING BY ALISTAIR ROACH

Printed and bound in Wales by
Gomer Press Limited, Ceredigion

British Library Cataloguing in Publication Data
A catalogue record for this book is available from the British Library

ISBN 978 0 956 2064 9 7

To my brother Alistair,
with affection and gratitude

ALSO IN MEMORY OF OUR PARENTS
ARTHUR KENNETH ROACH RNVR
(1913–1982) AND
DOROTHY LEONORA ROACH
(1913–2007)

AND OF OUR UNCLE
LIEUT. (E) BRYAN
CLEMENT JAMES ROACH RN
(1919–1941)
WHO DIED IN THE WARTIME
SINKING OF HMS *HOOD*

ACKNOWLEDGEMENTS

My gratitude to my brother Alistair Roach for the cover painting, and for all his help and advice with my research into the maritime aspects of this book. Also to Frank Cowin, who answered my initial questions about the *Serica* memorial tablet in Old Kirk Braddan, identified the grave of James Cubbin (I) at Malew, and has been helpful in many other ways; to James Cubbon of Half Moon Bay, California, great-great-grandson of Thomas Cubbin, for information about the family; to Charles Guard and members of the Manx Heritage Foundation for agreeing to publish the book; and to Ruth Sutherland, for her work on the cover design.

I must also acknowledge all the assistance I have been given by the patient and enthusiastic staff of the Manx National Heritage Library; the National Archives, Kew; the National Maritime Museum, Greenwich; the Merseyside Maritime Museum, Liverpool, and the Brunel Institute (ss *Great Britain* Trust), Bristol.

Special thanks to Kory Penney of the Maritime History Archive, Memorial University of Newfoundland; Graham Thompson of the National Maritime Museum; Ian Strawbridge of the National Archives; Janet Bishop of the New Brunswick Museum; Nathan Pendlebury, National Museums Liverpool; Roger Hull, Liverpool Record Office; Caroline Marrison Gill, Mersey Docks and Harbour Company; Valerie Harris, Daley Library, University of Illinois at Chicago; Edward Hood, School of Oriental & African Studies, University of London; Philippa Bassett, University of Birmingham Special Collections, and Helen Tookey, Liverpool University Press. Also to Midwest Production Services, Bartlett, Illinois, who copied to CD the recording of a radio lecture on Thomas Cubbin given by Professor Eugene B. Vest of the University of Illinois.

I have had useful conversations about my researches with Marion Bolam, Sandra Bolton, Nigel Crowe, Caroline McDonald and Geraldine Hampton, and am grateful to Isle of Man Newspapers and Priscilla Lewthwaite of the Isle of Man Family History Society for including (albeit in vain) my appeal for descendants of Thomas Cubbin in their respective publications.

Thanks also to all the friends – and indeed even my remotest acquaintances – who have patiently listened to me talking about Thomas Cubbin and the *Serica* for the past year; and last but not least, to my partner Robert Fyson and my daughter Anna Cottle for their unfailing love and support.

CONTENTS

FOREWORD

The World of Thomas Cubbin

11

*The Hurricane Wreck of
the ship 'Serica'*

51

AFTERWORD

116

Old Kirk Braddan dates in part as far back as the twelfth century.
Several of the Cubbin children were baptised here.

JUST A MILE from the outskirts of Douglas, modern capital of the Isle of Man, the church now known as 'Old' Kirk Braddan stands on a steeply sloping site, hemmed in by tightly-packed, moss-encrusted graves. At the top of the churchyard lies a freed slave. Further down, a huge stone obelisk commemorates a duke's son. Towards the bottom of the slope an old sea captain sleeps, at anchor at last, and not far away a small stone bears the stark inscription 'Cholera 1832'. Dark yews and cypresses grow in this place. In spring rooks nest in the trees, and the graves are surrounded by drifts of snowdrops.

There has been a church on the site for hundreds of years. Parts of the present building date back to the twelfth century; the tower, built in 1774, is the most recent addition. Inside the door stands a group of ancient cross slabs, one of them more than a thousand years old. There is a musicians' gallery, box pews, and the Island's only surviving three-decker pulpit.

Imposing marble slabs hang on the church walls, in memory of lofty dignitaries. But high on the south wall is a simple memorial tablet with an inscription on it that pierces the heart. It recalls the day in 1868 when two Manx children – eleven-year-old Tom Cubbin and his little brother James – died in the relentless surf on the eastern shore of Madagascar.

Tom and James, only twenty months old when he died, were the sons of a Manx master mariner, Thomas Cubbin, and his wife Mary. Their family's ordeal has gone down in the annals of seafaring, thanks to Thomas's own account, The Hurricane Wreck of the ship Serica, which was first published in 1870 and is reprinted here. But who was Thomas Cubbin, how did his wife and sons come to be on the coast of Madagascar with him, and what else lies behind this tragic story?

VALERIE COTTLE, DOUGLAS, ISLE OF MAN, 2011

Fishing boats on the beach below Mount Strange, between Derbyhaven and Castletown, from Glover's Illustrated Guide and Visitor's Companion through the Isle of Man, *1866. The young Thomas Cubbin would have walked past the Earl of Derby's ruined summerhouse on his way to school.*

COURTESY FRANK COWIN

FOREWORD

The World of Thomas Cubbin

Thomas Cubbin was born in the fishing hamlet of Derbyhaven near Castletown, the old capital of the Isle of Man, on 20th February 1823. The occupation of his father, also Thomas, would later be given as 'shoemaker', but it is likely that he was a fisherman as well. As a child young Thomas had the sandy beaches and rocky shoreline of the peninsula of Langness to play on, two busy little harbours and a ruined fort and chapel on nearby St Michael's Isle to explore. And when he was old enough to make his way along the shore to school in Castletown, less than a mile away, the towering limestone castle, the market square, and the strutting soldiers to be seen there, would have fascinated a lively and inquisitive boy.

By the time Thomas was born, Castletown had been for six centuries the seat of the Island's Governor, the place where its unelected parliament – the House of Keys – sat, where law courts were held, where the soldiers of the garrison could be watched on parade, and where country people crowded in through the narrow streets on Saturdays to sell their produce in the market. The Governor's presence made this a fashionable town; fine houses were being built, balls were held in the assembly rooms, and sacred concerts in the garrison church of St Mary's. Dorothy Wordsworth, passing through on a tour of the Island in 1826, described the 'drawbridge, river and castle, handsome strong fortress, soldiers pacing sentinel, officers and music, groups of women in white caps listening, very like a town in French Flanders'.

Castle Rushen and Castletown harbour, by George Pickering, 1832.

Castletown's population of just over two thousand included many of the Island's most important citizens – advocates, clergy and other officials, retired military and naval men, surgeons and 'academic professors', even a 'professor of dancing'. As well as the houses lining its narrow streets, the town was packed with shops and businesses: drapers, boot and shoemakers, spirit dealers, ships' chandlers, tobacconists, wine merchants and hairdressers. The most popular inn was the newly-rebuilt George Hotel ('chaise and carriages of every description, saddle horses, etc.'), opposite the castle, but in 1823 the town's drinkers had a choice of no fewer than twenty-eight public houses.

Castletown's harbour was never capable of accommodating vessels of any great size; the primacy of Douglas in that regard, which eventually would lead to its taking over as the Island's capital, was already grudgingly acknowledged. But when Thomas Cubbin was old enough to go to school in Castletown, there would have been much in and around the area of the harbour for an adventurous boy to look at, and to learn.

At the time of his birth the town had one particularly famous resident. In the Isle of Man the hero of the Battle of Trafalgar has never been considered to be Horatio Nelson, but rather John Quilliam, the Manx farmer's son who, as first lieutenant on board the *Victory*, rigged up a makeshift steering gear after her wheel had been shot away, and thus made Nelson's victory possible. On his return home to the Island Quilliam served two periods of duty in the House of Keys, married a local heiress, Margaret Christian Stevenson, and for the last twelve years of his life divided his time between the home she had inherited a few miles from Castletown, and his own fine Balcony House on the Parade in the town centre. A story circulated that he had the main chimney flue constructed especially to encourage the wind to whistle down it and remind him of his years at sea.

The hero of Trafalgar took a keen interest in the Manx fishing fleet, and kept a fishing smack of his own at Derbyhaven. He suggested improvements to include the building of a breakwater in the shallow bay, and even the cutting of a canal across the narrow isthmus of Langness from there to Castletown. Quilliam died in 1829, aged fifty-seven, when Thomas Cubbin was six years old. Was Thomas as a child ever lifted onto his father's shoulders for a glimpse of him? As he grew up, memories of Quilliam might have been inspirational for a boy thinking of a career at sea.

In 1822 a National School had been opened in Castletown, and by the end of the decade Thomas may well have been amongst its pupils. Its existence had arisen from an initiative of 1819, when 'several of the respectable inhabitants of Castletown, observing and lamenting the state of the morals of the lowest orders of the people of the town and neighbourhood, and being convinced that it arose from a want of religious instruction for youth, determined to use their utmost endeavour to correct the evil'. These worthy citizens asked the Society for Promoting Christian Knowledge to supply them with books, and regularly examined their pupils for proficiency in reading, spelling, mathematics and the catechism. In later life, and in the way he brought up his own children, Thomas would still show signs of his pious upbringing. Since 1799 there had also been a school in Douglas Street, the Taubman Endowed School for Boys, which by the 1830s was advertising itself as teaching navigation; he could also have spent some time as a pupil there.

Thomas Cubbin first went to sea as an apprentice in 1839, when he was sixteen years old. When he entered his apprenticeship as a seaman he was described as being five foot seven-and-a-half inches tall, and having sandy auburn hair and blue-grey eyes. He may in due course have grown taller, but perhaps he was always a stocky man; years later, after weeks of near-starvation following the loss of the *Serica*, he would complain that 'in the reduced condition I was in, my weight could not be much over twelve stone'.

Why would he choose to go into the merchant service, rather than following the footsteps of John Quilliam into the Royal Navy? The end of the Napoleonic Wars in 1815 had seen a change of role for the Navy, from fighting force to peacekeeper. In 1815 there had been more than 700 ships in commission, and 140,000 men; within three years these numbers had been reduced to 130 ships and 19,000 men. The Navy was to see little aggressive action until the Crimean War in the 1850s, and even then shore bombardment, rather than sea warfare, was the order of the day. When Thomas was growing up, the Isle of Man was flooded with retired half-pay military and naval officers.

However, the role the Royal Navy was to play so vitally during much of the nineteenth century was that of protecting Victoria's burgeoning Empire and its worldwide trade. Since the mid-eighteenth century, the British Government had been gradually extending its control over the previously all-powerful East India Company; in 1813 the company was deprived of its monopoly of trade with India, and in 1833 of its remaining monopolies. The seas were now wide open, and the new industries created in the north-west of England were hungry for fresh markets. By the time Thomas was ready to go out into the world, the merchant service was the place for an ambitious young man to be – the place where he might hope to make his fortune.

So Thomas signed his indentures as a merchant seaman, and was bound for four years into an apprenticeship which would put him on track to becoming an officer, and eventually master of his own ship. This was the route which would take him up the ladder of achievement, even if his parents had to struggle to pay for his indentures. Unlike a ship's 'boy', who really did start at the bottom and might climb no further than becoming an AB, the apprentice seaman was destined from his earliest days for higher things.

This could be taken literally, as the first test imposed on any apprentice was to be sent aloft into the ship's rigging, something sailors had to do hundreds of times on every voyage. A terrifying experience for a novice, it could involve climbing 200 feet or more up the rigging and then lying along the yards, feet on a footrope, to reef or furl the sails. This manoeuvre took both hands, and might have to be performed high above the deck of a wildly pitching and yawing vessel, even in pitch darkness. A boy who failed the test could never hope to make a career as a seaman. A fall onto the deck would involve serious injury or death, and a plunge into the sea would almost inevitably mean drowning. It was not easy to turn a sailing vessel around to rescue a man who had gone overboard.

Typical was the case of apprentice Daniel Dickinson, who in 1865 fell to his death in the sea from the barque *Ehen*, off the west coast of Patagonia. 'An extraordinary fine lad', Daniel was on his first voyage and two days short of his fifteenth birthday. The captain, who had turned the ship round but was unable to save him, recorded that 'his friends, especially his mother, were strongly averse to his going to sea; but he was bent upon doing so, and to the inexpressible grief of his friends, the first has also unhappily proved to be his last voyage'.

An apprentice had to learn the name of every sail and rope, and where to find it at any time of the day or night, even if the ship was heaving and awash under breaking waves. Every day, so long as it was not impossibly stormy, the junior members of the crew would be found on their knees 'holystoning' the deck with pumice and seawater to prevent it becoming slippery. And every day the bilges would have to be pumped out by hand. When Thomas first went to sea most ships were still built of wood, and all wooden ships took in water continuously, to a greater or lesser extent. The bilges would have to be emptied by means of a two-man pump, to the accompaniment – as with so many other tasks at sea – of the rhythmic singing of sea shanties.

On long voyages, apart from their ration of poor-quality meat and dried peas, all crew below officer level lived largely on hard tack, or ship's biscuit. Thomas would have had to learn to stomach this simple mixture of flour and water, sometimes flavoured with a little salt, which was baked so hard as to be indestructible for years. This, of course, depended on it being kept dry. It could be deliberately softened for eating by being dipped into a hot drink, or even melted into a kind of porridge, but if it got damp in storage it was often found to be infested with weevils. 'Maggot-racing' was said to be a popular pastime amongst apprentice seamen.

The apprentices did not mix with the rest of the crew, except when they were actually working together, and certainly could not socialise with them ashore – Thomas would have been banned from drinking alcohol or indeed from visiting alehouses for the entire period of his apprenticeship. In many ways apprentices had a harder time than the ordinary crew, because they were seen as always being in some sense on the side of the officers. By signing his indentures Thomas had been bound to instant obedience to any order from a ship's officer. He had also promised to keep a true account of any money or goods which might come into his hands, to pay over to his master any wages or prize money he might earn if he entered the Royal Navy during his apprenticeship, to refrain from damaging his master's interests or allowing others to damage them, not to waste or embezzle his master's goods, or to absent himself from service without leave, or to play 'unlawful games'. It is not known whether the pastime of maggot-racing came under this last heading.

The master, on his side, committed himself to teach the apprentice the business of a seaman, to provide him with food, drink, lodging, medicine and surgical assistance, and to pay him an incremental wage over the years of his apprenticeship. Thomas would have had to supply his own bedding, clothing and personal requirements when on board. The surety which his parents had paid when he signed his indentures would be forfeited if he failed to stay the course.

The first steamship had crossed the Atlantic before Thomas Cubbin was born, and by the time he was three years old a small steamer was making the weekly return trip between Douglas and Whitehaven. Later in his career he would sail in vessels powered by a combination of sail with steam, and in screw-driven steamships. But he was very much a man of the great age of sail, with all the knowledge and experience that went with it. Steamships might not be dependent on winds or currents, and their masters could choose the most direct routes, but they were encumbered by the weight and bulk of their own heavy fuel. Improved sail technology, and the navigational skills of the masters of ships like the mighty clipper *Thermopylae*, made record-breaking voyages possible throughout the nineteenth century. The *Thermopylae* took just sixty days to sail from London to Melbourne in 1868, with nothing to power her but the wind.

A Manxman with ambitions to sail deep sea would naturally make his way across the Irish Sea to Liverpool, and so it was with Thomas Cubbin. Once there, he would have been plunged into a world unimaginable to a boy from Castletown, however many people had tried to describe it to him. Already this great, turbulent, monstrous port had been hailed as the 'second city of Empire', and during Thomas's working life the city and its network of docks would grow out of all recognition. By the 1850s it was claimed that Liverpool was linked by trade to 'every port of any importance in every quarter of the globe'.

In the early nineteenth century Liverpool had replaced London as England's premier port for importing cotton, firstly from the West Indies and later from the United States; huge fortunes were already being made by the city's cotton merchants. Sugar came in from the West Indies, grain from Ireland, timber from Canada, silks and spices, ceramics and ivories from China... The landward side of the docks along the east bank of the Mersey was lined with flour mills, sugar refineries, tobacco warehouses, and factories to process dairy products and live-

Bird's eye view of the Liverpool and Birkenhead Docks, by John Isaac, 1859. The Serica sailed on her fateful voyage from Birkenhead (top left) on 7th December 1867.

stock. And the opening of the Liverpool & Manchester Railway in 1830 meant that goods manufactured in the factories of the north-west of England could be brought to the docks and sent straight out around the world. Later on, thousands of emigrants would be added to the traffic through the port; in the peak year of 1852, 299,099 – often desperate – English, Irish and Europeans left Liverpool for America, on over a thousand sailings.

The most vivid account of dock life in mid-nineteenth century Liverpool is to be found in Herman Melville's novel *Redburn*, published in 1849 and based on some months the American writer had spent in the great port city ten years earlier. Melville describes how lonely and isolated the life of a sailor could be. Sitting in a smoke-filled Liverpool tavern, and thinking of all the famous places he has heard of in England, his hero realises:

> ...that my prospects of seeing the world as a sailor were, after all, but very doubt-ful; for sailors only go round the world, without going into it; and their reminis-cences of travel are only a dim recollection of a chain of tap-rooms surrounding the globe, parallel with the Equator. They but touch the perimeter of the circle; hover about the edges of terra-firma; and only land upon wharves and pier-heads...

Did Thomas realise this when he first went to sea? Would he be content to 'go round the world, without going into it'? Would he have been apprehensive if he had grasped the idea, or was the prospect of an unfettered life at sea part of the attraction? Of all the cities he would get to know in the course of his seafaring life – from North and South America to Africa, from India to China, Australia and New Zealand – Liverpool would for much of the time be his home port. And as he got to know it he would, like so many before and since, have grown to loathe and love the place in equal measure. Melville paints a fearsome picture of the city's dangers, but also remembers how fondly seamen embrace it:

> ...of all sea-ports in the world, Liverpool, perhaps, most abounds in all the vari-ety of land-sharks, land-rats, and other vermin, which make the hapless mariner their prey. In the shape of landlords, bar-keepers, clothiers, crimps, and boarding-house loungers, the land-sharks devour him, limb by limb; while the land-rats and mice constantly nibble at his purse.

Other perils he runs, also, far worse; from the denizens of notorious Corinthian haunts in the vicinity of the docks, which in depravity are not to be matched by any thing this side of the pit that is bottomless.

And yet, sailors love this Liverpool; and upon long voyages to distant parts of the globe, will be continually dilating upon its charms and attractions, and extolling it above all other seaports in the world. For in Liverpool they find their Paradise – not the well known street of that name – and one of them told me he would be content to lie in Prince's Dock till he hove up anchor for the world to come.

The building of Liverpool's dock estate had been necessitated in the first place by the huge tidal rise and fall – as much as thirty-three feet – in the Mersey. The creation of enclosed docks, built out from the original shore line, enabled vessels to remain afloat at all states of the tide, and at the same time allowed them, and their valuable cargoes, to be kept secure. The first, the so-called 'Old Dock', the first enclosed maritime dock in the world, had been built as early as 1715. By 1840 docks stretched for more than four miles along the east bank of the river; eventually there would be no fewer than fifty dock basins, extending for seven miles, with an additional network of basins on the Birkenhead bank which was begun in 1844. It was from Birkenhead that Thomas and Mary Cubbin would set out on their fateful voyage in the *Serica* in 1867.

Each dock was between ten and fifteen acres in extent, with access for dockers and wagons via gateways on the landward side. From *Redburn* again:

> ...upon their being closed, the whole dock is shut up like a house. From the river, the entrance is through a water-gate, and ingress to ships is only to be had, when the level of the dock coincides with that of the river; that is, about the time of high tide, as the level of the dock is always at that mark. So that when it is low tide in the river, the keels of the ships enclosed by the quays are elevated more than twenty feet above those of the vessels in the stream. This, of course, produces a striking effect to the stranger, to see hundreds of immense ships floating high aloft in the heart of a mass of masonry.

For young Thomas Cubbin from Derbyhaven, who had only ever seen open tidal harbours with vessels lying in them like beached whales for half the day, such sights must have seemed near-miraculous. He would have marvelled at the skills needed to manoeuvre large sailing ships in and out of the docks, to reach

'*Canada Timber Docks towards the Close of Day*' by Robert Dudley, 1870s. The Canada Dock was opened in 1858, when Canada was the source of most of Britain's timber. The Estelle *arrived here from* New Brunswick in 1863. Thomas Cubbin bought her four years later, changing her name to Serica. Here can be seen some of the city's draught horses at work, and Herman Melville's '*hundreds of immense ships floating high aloft in the heart of a mass of masonry*'.

their berths in safety. Outside each water-gate was a basin, entered through a narrow gap between stone pier heads. Here ships would lie waiting their turn to come in; in due course a dock master would come aboard to direct operations, hailing the crews of other vessels and shouting instructions so as to avoid collisions. And the noise! The raucous shouts of sailors in a myriad languages, the crashing of crates and bales onto paved wharves, the grind of iron-bound wagon wheels, the sparking hooves of the great patient drayhorses – all these sounds would have been amplified as they echoed off the high walls. From *Redburn*:

> Surrounded by its broad belt of masonry, each Liverpool dock is a walled town, full of life and commotion; or rather, it is a small archipelago, an epitome of the world, where all the nations of Christendom, and even those of Heathendom, are represented. For, in itself, each ship is an island, a floating colony of the tribe to which it belongs.
>
> Here are brought together the remotest limits of the earth; and in the collective spars and timbers of these ships, all the forests of the globe are represented, as in a grand parliament of masts. Canada and New Zealand send their pines; America her live oak; India her teak; Norway her spruce; and the Right Honorable Mahogany, member for Honduras and Campeachy, is seen at his post by the wheel. Here, under the beneficent sway of the Genius of Commerce, all climes and countries embrace; and yard-arm touches yard-arm in brotherly love.

By the time he was twenty-two Thomas had signed on as Second Mate on the *Mona*, which had been built in the Isle of Man but was Liverpool-registered. Between February 1844 and January 1845 her master, Wilfred Lawson, took her from Liverpool to Batavia in Java, and probably to other ports in the former Dutch East Indies as well; this was an important source of spices for the western world, and of sugar, coffee, and commodities like the notorious Batavian 'Arrack' or rum. A newspaper report for October 1844 mentions that 'The *Trusty* from Adelaide had taken a cargo of sugar and coffee at Batavia, and left for London on the 17th August. The *Mona* was loading there for England'. The *Mona* eventually returned to London, and within three months Thomas had enlisted as Second Mate on the 306-ton barque *Mary Elizabeth*. She sailed out of Liverpool on 25th April 1845 and headed for Bombay, already a vital hub for the world's cotton trade. This time Thomas was at sea for over a year, as the *Mary Elizabeth* did not return to England until 28th June 1846. Two months after that he was Mate on the *Landford,* setting sail on 11th August 1846 and not returning until 19th May 1847. This time we know neither the destination nor the cargoes carried. He went to sea again almost immediately, spending just three months, from June to September 1847, as Mate on the *Sherbrooke,* which was registered in Cork and probably a transatlantic emigrant ship.

Thomas had good reason for being back in Liverpool by the autumn of 1847, for he, unlike some of his fellow-mariners, was not destined to spend his life as a lonely wanderer on the world's oceans. On 27th October, aged twenty-four, he married twenty-year-old Mary Ann Wagstaff at St Mark's Church in Upper Duke Street. Mary was the daughter of another mariner, John Wagstaff, and would play a central part not only in Thomas's personal life, but also in his seafaring career. She often sailed with him; on the first page of *The Wreck of the Serica,* he writes, 'My wife was not ignorant of a sea-faring life ... we had previously sailed long and successfully together'.

The lives of women who spent time on the ships of the Royal Navy, either openly or clandestinely, is well documented; less so the lives of the nineteenth century wives and families – on this side of the Atlantic at least – who lived at sea on merchant naval vessels. They seem to have existed as far as possible as if they were at home on land: caring for the personal needs of their husbands, children, and any pet animals on board, mending and making clothes and toys, dispensing medicine, sometimes doing a little baking (the crew would be fed by the ship's cook), reading, writing letters, keeping a diary, sketching or keeping up other hobbies. They would be isolated for months on end from others of their own sex, so 'speaking' a ship which had another captain's wife on board would be quite an occasion. But what is indubitable is that, when required, such women could show enormous courage and resourcefulness.

By the time Thomas and Mary lost the *Serica* they had been married for more than twenty years. In *The Wreck of the Serica* he gives a touching description of her courage as they battle together against the worst ordeal of their lives: 'She is only a delicate creature to look upon ... but ... although she suffered so much, I found her good spirit had not forsaken her; and I firmly believe she had more courage than any one of the boat's crew'. Mary not only endured appalling phys-

St Mark's Church, Upper Duke Street, Liverpool, where Thomas Cubbin married Mary Ann Wagstaff on 27th October 1847. The church was demolished in 1913 after the Anglican Cathedral was built nearby. From T. Troughton, History of Liverpool, 1810.

LIVERPOOL RECORD OFFICE

By The Lords of the Committee of Privy Council for Trade.

Certificate of Competency
as
MASTER.

To Thomas Cubbins.

Whereas it has been reported to us that you have been found duly qualified to fulfil the duties of Master in the Merchant Service we do hereby in pursuance of the Mercantile Marine Act 1850 grant you this Certificate of Competency.

Given under the Seal of The Board of Trade, this Second day of January 1852.

By order of the Board
Countersigned.

Officers of the Naval Department

Entered at the General Register and Record Office of Seamen, on the Third day of January 1852.

Thomas Cubbin's Master's Certificate, awarded in Liverpool by the Board of Trade in 1852; as usual in the English context, his surname is spelled with a final 's'.

NATIONAL MARITIME MUSEUM

ical suffering, but she stood up bravely to thieving and mutinous crew members as Thomas battled to save their precious ship.

Thomas was at sea almost continuously for several years after his marriage. From January to August 1848 he was Mate on the Liverpool-registered 659-ton *Majestic*, en route for 'Africa' (country unspecified). From 6th November that year until 30th November 1849 he was Chief Mate on the *Indus*, registered in Liverpool but on that occasion sailing out of London. On 14th January 1850 he sailed as Mate of the *Wilson*, across the Atlantic from Liverpool to Maranham on the north-east coast of Brazil, returning four months later. The purpose of the voyage is unknown. In the same year the House of Commons Select Committee on the African Slave Trade commissioned the publication of a map of this coastal region of Brazil, indicating 'places where slavers land their cargoes and also where they are fitted out for slave trading'. Slavery had been abolished throughout the British Empire in 1833, but it was rife in the Portuguese colonies until much later in the century. There is no reason to think that Thomas had anything personally to do with it. We know from *The Wreck of the Serica* that he saw slaves auctioned during his seafaring career, and that he disliked the trade:

> I have witnessed slave sales by auction, and it seemed very cruel to see intending purchasers handling them as dealers would a horse or a cow in our own country, with only one exception; here intending purchasers would take the animal by the jaw to examine the mouth; the slave was told to show his ivory.

The year 1852 was an important one, for on 2nd January Thomas received his full Master's Certificate from the Board of Trade (he had been awarded the provisional 2nd Class version in 1850). But the first command that we know of did not come until three years later, when he took charge of the 597-ton clipper *Rock City*. Joseph Conrad, that incomparable chronicler of the seas, says of his character Captain Allistoun in *The Nigger of the Narcissus* that his 'secret ambition was to make her accomplish some day a brilliantly quick passage which would be mentioned in nautical papers'. Thomas Cubbin started his career as master with just such a record-breaking run. On 4th June 1855 he brought the *Rock City* into Auckland, New Zealand, with passengers and cargo from London, having completed the journey against the odds in only eighty-eight days. The *Daily*

Southern Cross of 5th June reported, 'The clipper ship *Rock City*, Capt. Cubbins [*sic*] arrived in our harbour on Sunday last. She has made one of the shortest, if not the shortest, passages ever made to New Zealand; the run out being accomplished in 88 days from the Downs. The *Rock City* sailed from Gravesend on the 4th of March, and the Downs on the 6th. The *Rock City* is a British North American built vessel. She brings 19 passengers and about 850 tons of cargo for this port'.

The *Rock City* had been built in St John, Brunswick, by James Smith, also the builder of the famous emigrant clipper *Marco Polo*. When Thomas was first master she was only on her second voyage. From Gravesend he had reached the equator within twenty-two days, but was becalmed for five days off the coast of Brazil. Deep in the South Atlantic he had passed within sight of the towering Gough Island, and after that, sailing on the 'great circle' principle, had taken the *Rock City* into the high southern latitudes and encountered masses of floating ice and large icebergs.

Before the vessel left Auckland he had one regrettable duty to attend to. The steward, James Bruce, had gone missing on a Saturday night, together with the ship's longboat, and Thomas himself set out to look for him. The harbourmaster told him that his brother had seen something he thought might be a Maori canoe, with a man paddling it, drifting towards the offshore island of Rangitoto. Thomas found Bruce late the following evening, lying 'quite dead' in the longboat on the island's volcanic rocks. The body was brought back to Auckland so that an inquest could be held. In his evidence Thomas affirmed, 'I know no reason why the steward should wish to leave the ship; there had been no quarrel with him; no one else was absent at the time; there were no oars in the boat; he always appeared satisfied with the ship'. The verdict was 'Found dead in the longboat of the *Rock City*: cause of death, exhaustion'. It must have been a deeply depressing business.

On 8th August the *Nelson Examiner and New Zealand Chronicle* recorded the *Rock City*'s arrival there: 'Arrived – August 6, ship *Rock City*, 600, Cubbins, from New Plymouth, with a general cargo for that port'. And three days later, 'the ship *Rock City*, which put in here on Sunday, is transferring her Taranaki cargo to the *Admiral Napier*. The *Rock City* was off Taranaki eleven days without being able to discharge the cargo which she had brought from London for that port (the remainder of her cargo had previously been discharged in Auckland), when, seeing no prospect of a favourable change in the weather, Captain Cubbins ran for Nelson. The *Rock City* is a remarkable vessel, and proceeds hence to China'.

The eldest of Thomas and Mary Cubbin's surviving children, Esther Charlotte, had been born in Liverpool earlier in 1855, surprisingly not until eight years after their marriage; this may have been partly attributable to Thomas's long absences at sea, or possibly Mary had suffered a series of stillbirths or miscarriages. Of the eight children we know of, either three or four were born at sea, and Mary and little Esther could well have been on this voyage to New Zealand. The Cubbins' first son Tom was born in 1856, probably also on board the *Rock City*, which was under Thomas's command until 1857.

On 8th December that year he sailed out of Liverpool as master of a much larger vessel, the 1,279-ton *Caribou*, en route for Port Phillip in Australia (the settlement further inland had been given its name of Melbourne just twenty years earlier). Whether Mary and the two children sailed with him is not recorded, but it seems very likely that they did. It was a route he had sailed before on the *Rock City*, as usual taking his vessel deep down towards the Antarctic to catch, not merely the Roaring Forties, but the so-called Furious Fifties, powerful westerly winds which enabled the captains of clipper ships to make the quickest possible passage to the Antipodes. Further south again could be found the Screaming Sixties, but only the most daring or foolhardy masters would risk their vessels in the atrocious conditions of that region. On this occasion Thomas was to make a surprising discovery. On 13th March 1858 he wrote from Hobson's Bay, Auckland, New Zealand, to the Admiralty in London, to report a previously uncharted land:

> I sailed from Liverpool on the 8th December, 1857, bound to Port Phillip, in Australia. On February 22, wind westerly, brisk gale, with snow squalls; at 10.33 a.m. in a clear between the squalls I fancied I saw land to the southward; took in studding-sails, shortened sail, and stood towards it. At 1.30 p.m. hove-to abreast the island, with the centre bearing S.S.W., about twelve miles, lowered a life-boat, and sent her to land. I afterwards stood in to about nine miles off shore, and got no ground with 120 fathoms of line. The island appeared to be in a S.E. and N.W.

direction, about twenty-five miles, its southern extreme landing to the S.W., forming a deep bight on its western side, which was entirely snow-clad and gave it the appearance of a great barrier of ice. The greater part of the whole island was covered with snow. There was a remarkable group of high rocks lying off to the N.E. from the S.E. part of the island, apparently six or seven miles, and on the N.W. extreme, an iceberg aground. The island was cloud-capped, but I think that its greatest elevation could not be less than 450 feet above the level of the sea. Whilst hove-to, I was astonished to see vessels at anchor in a bay, we having opened it through drifting to the S.E. One of them got under weigh and stood towards it; it proved to be the American schooner *Oxford*, of Fairhaven. They put out a boat and the master came on board; he told me they called it Kurds Island, and that it was discovered by them eighteen months before. He seemed annoyed my boat had landed, and advised me to go and leave her behind, saying that she would never return, but I told him I would never leave her while I had another boat to seek for her. I was very anxious, for it was then sundown, and darkness coming on fast; but while speaking, the look-out at the mast head reported the boat in sight. He then became more communicative, and told me they were after oil, that the shores of the island swarmed with sea elephants, and that they had sent to America from the island, since the discovery, 25,000 barrels of oil. The island was bold on the north-east side, and no hidden dangers; and the bay where they lay was a fine bay or natural harbour – no sunken dangers – with twelve to twenty fathoms all over, and sheltered from all winds except a north-easterly, with a fine river of fresh water at the head of it. He also told me that there was another island west of Kurds, distant some thirty miles, and another E.S.E. seventy miles, both of which he had seen but never landed on. My own officers that were in the boat confirmed his statement of the sea elephants, and the island being well watered; there were penguins and other birds in myriads, and on an island about a mile apart from the main appeared to be a great mound of guano. Whilst lying to, I went to look at my abstract, and it made me shudder to think that only twelve months before I ran past the island at midnight in a heavy gale of wind, not more than four or five miles distant, ignorant of its existence. My greatest wish, on sending my boat to the island, was to find out if there were any shipwrecked persons on it whom I might relieve. The island was entirely of volcanic origin, my six officers having found the surface ashes and stones.

Thomas's account was published by New Zealand's *Colonist* newspaper on 14th September 1858, under the heading CURIOUS DISCOVERY IN THE SOUTH

ATLANTIC. The *Age* of Melbourne, carrying an abbreviated version on 11th March 1859, gave the coordinates of his uncharted island as 53°1'S, 73°7' E, which would identify the island group with Heard's (or Heard, as it is now known) Island, and the nearby McDonalds. Either Thomas, or one of the officers he sent ashore, must have mis-heard the name as 'Kurds'. There are few places on earth more remote: Heard Island is nearly 2,500 miles southwest of Australia, 3,000 miles southeast of Africa, and more than 600 miles north of Antarctica.

In fact a whole series of mariners thought they had made the first sighting of this desolate volcanic outcrop, from Captain Cook in 1773 through other possible sightings by British and American masters in 1833 and 1848. But it had been officially discovered on 25th November 1853, by an American sealer, Captain John Heard of the *Oriental*, en route from Boston to Melbourne. He reported it a month later, and claimed the right to have it named it after himself. John Heard's wife was definitely on board the *Oriental*, for she was the first to describe the island:

> At 10 o'clock the Captain was walking on deck and saw what he supposed to be an immense iceberg ... the atmosphere was hazy, and then a heavy snow squall came up which shut it out entirely from our view. Not long after the sun shone again, and I went up again and with the glass, tried to get an outline of it to sketch its form. The sun seemed so dazzling on the water, and the tops of the apparent icebergs covered with snow; the outline was very indistinct. We were all the time nearing the object and on looking again the Captain pronounced it to be land. The Island is not laid down on the chart, neither is it in the Epitome, so we are perhaps the discoverers ... I think it must be a twin to Desolation Island, it is certainly a frigid looking place.

When Thomas Cubbin arrived at Heard Island on the *Caribou*, the killing and rendering of elephant seals for their oil was at its height, and by the following year the majority of them had been slaughtered by gangs of men specially landed for the purpose. An early observer wrote that the seals were 'sometimes treated with horrible brutality'. By the time the trade ended in 1877 some forty vessels, almost all from America, had made more than 100 voyages to Heard; their discarded iron melting pots and oil barrels are still to be seen there.

There is no doubt that Mary and Thomas were together on the next journey of which we have a record, for during the two-year voyage she gave birth to two children. They set out from London on a smaller vessel, the 324-ton wooden barque *Ocean Gem,* on 6th July 1861, once more en route for China. Since Mary was already six months pregnant, it is no surprise to find that she took a personal maid with her to help care for the expected baby. Twenty-four year old Mary Ann Fleming from Bermondsey had never been to sea before, but she loyally completed the round trip. Mary Cubbin gave birth to a son, James, on 25th October 1861, when the *Ocean Gem* was southwest of Australia.

This long voyage, with Amoy in China's Fujian province as its ultimate destination, did not pass smoothly. Amongst his crew Thomas had recruited two seventeen-year-old youths, both of whom had only just completed the first year of their apprenticeships. Neither of them could have been described as 'an extraordinary fine lad'. One, Charles Thomas, jumped ship before they even left London. And there was a more serious incident en route: when they were five months into their voyage and in the South China Sea, Thomas had to record a case of flagrant insubordination in his log. On 6th December 1861 he wrote:

> William Emms was at the helm and had the ship all in the wind. I was below at the time. The Second Mate was reducing the after-sail. I heard him call to the man at the helm several times if the ship was going off. He made no reply until he had been asked a number of times it was as tho' he had called to a dog. I went up and spoke to him of his conduct and he became insolent and used most provoking language. I ordered him several times to hold his peace. He said he would not – I told him if he did not I would punish him. He defied me to do so. I then pulled him away from the helm. He struck me several times, kicked and made all the resistance in his power. I took him below and put him in irons with bread and water for his fare. I have had occasion to talk to him many times of his insolent conduct to the officers, all the crew seem to take pleasure in doing so.

In a note on 17th December, presumably when Emms was released from his irons, Thomas recorded that when this entry was read over to him he denied it and unrepentantly 'used insolent language and provoking. He said he had been very much abused, more than any other man in the ship. When I asked him who by he said me. I asked him in what way, he said I looked at him with my nose turned up...' William Emms could not be discharged until the *Ocean Gem* reached Shanghai six months later, on 3rd May 1862. Whether his behaviour improved in any way is not recorded.

Conrad, again in *The Nigger of the Narcissus*, writes, 'Discipline is not ceremonious in merchant ships, where the sense of hierarchy is weak, and where all feel themselves equal before the unconcerned immensity of the sea...' Emms was an AB, a twenty-four year old Londoner, and for him to strike his captain was a grave offence. It was not, however, the gravest. Under Board of Trade regulations governing the merchant navy at this period, punishment for misdemeanours mostly involved the docking of pay. The least serious offence, for which half a day's pay would be forfeited, was for a seaman to fail to bring up and air his bedding when ordered to do so. A day's pay would be docked for quarrelling, swearing, smoking below decks, carrying a sheath knife, profaning the sabbath, or using insolent language towards the master or mate. The ship's cook could be fined one day's pay for failing to have a crew meal ready at the appointed time.

Not being on board at the time agreed for the start of a voyage would lose a seaman two days' pay, as would sleeping, or any other form of serious negligence, while on look-out. Bringing spirits on board was punishable by the loss of three days' pay. But by far the worst offence was secreting contraband goods on board with intent to smuggle: for this a seaman would lose a whole month's pay. Officers would be fined twice as heavily as seamen for an identical offence. William Emms would have had his wages docked when he was paid off in Shanghai, as well as being locked in irons on bread and water for ten days during the voyage.

Thomas's second apprentice, John Edward Clegg, made it as far as Shanghai, but deserted there on 26th April 1862. And on 5th May there was another deserter, the thirty-four year old AB Richard Prior. This port, already growing rapidly, was perhaps a particularly tempting place in which to jump ship. The *Ocean Gem* seems to have spent two or three months there, until Thomas found another cargo and took her on to her final destination in July. Amoy (modern Xiamen) was, and still is, one of the busiest port cities in Fujian. It was closed to outside trade during the eighteenth century, but then re-opened as a Treaty Port in 1842, and after that was much used by overseas traders. The offshore island of

Gulang Yu was allotted to foreigners and developed in European style; Thomas and Mary would have felt quite at home there.

In August they took the *Ocean Gem* south to Hong Kong. Most of the original crew had been paid off and new ones recruited in Shanghai and Amoy, but here they completed their complement for the journey home. The last recruit was a twenty-eight year old Norwegian, Hans Kristoffersen, taken on as the ship's carpenter. But before long Kristoffersen became ill. The *Ocean Gem*'s log records that he died of dysentery in Ningpo on 2nd November. This was puzzlingly further north than the course Thomas might have been expected to take, but he may have deviated there in order to get help for the sick man.

Shortly after they left Hong Kong, Mary became pregnant again. The Cubbins' second daughter, another Mary, was born in the deep southern reaches of the Indian Ocean, at 2.40am on 26th June 1863, as the *Ocean Gem* made her way back towards England.

These must have been profitable voyages, for by the time they reached home in June 1863 Thomas seems to have amassed quite a considerable fortune. In the September of that year he and Mary were in a position to spend £1,150 on a 'mansion' three miles outside Douglas, the largest port and main town – shortly to become the capital – of the Isle of Man. Although this is the word their conveyance used, 'mansion' is rather an exaggeration, but Rose Hill was a substantial square house in a magnificent position high above the main road from Douglas to Castletown, with views down into Douglas Bay and across to the Island's northern hills. Thomas even erected a flagstaff, from which he no doubt proudly flew the Red Ensign of the merchant service. The property came with fifteen acres of land, and they spent another £665 on additional tenanted fields.

Within a few weeks of the purchase of their fine new home, however, there came a grievous blow. Little James, who had started life on board the *Ocean Gem* deep in the Southern Ocean just two years earlier, died suddenly. In their grief they took him to be buried not at Kirk Braddan, but with other members of Thomas's family in the graveyard at Kirk Malew. There is a white marble tablet at ground level in the outer north-eastern angle of the church walls with the inscription 'Sacred to the memory of James, son of Thomas Cubbon [sic] and Mary Ann his wife. Born at sea October 25th 1861. Died October 27th 1863'.

Douglas Bay, with the entrance to the harbour, by George Pickering, 1849. The Cubbin family lived at Rose Hill, Braddan, which has a similarly splendid view of the northern hills, from 1863 to 1875.

Thomas and Mary lost their younger son, James, shortly after his second birthday in 1863 (the James who died in Madagascar was named after him). They had only just bought Rose Hill, which may explain why his grave is at Malew, the burial ground of Thomas's family, rather than Braddan which would soon become their parish church.

Esther (always known as Etty) was now aged eight, and the Cubbins had seven-year-old Tom, and the latest addition to their family, three-month-old Mary. Three further children – Jane, another James (called, as was often the Victorian custom although a strange one to us, after his dead brother), and Amy Mona would come along by 1867.

Jane and Amy were both born in the Isle of Man, but it is not possible to be certain about the second James. According to the record on the memorial tablet of his age at the time he died, his birth must have been in May 1866. This date does not tally with a time when the Cubbins are known to have been at sea, yet he was not baptised at Kirk Braddan until 2nd June 1867, when he was more than a year old. In *The Wreck of the Serica* Thomas describes Tom ambiguously as 'the elder of three, ocean-born'. Does this mean that he was the eldest of three *sons* born at sea, Tom and the two Jameses, or the eldest of three ocean-born *children* – Tom, the first James, and Mary?

Within three months of buying Rose Hill Thomas was back at sea again, and engaged in a very different kind of voyage from anything he had undertaken before. On this occasion he would certainly have left Mary and the children behind at Rose Hill, for he had agreed to take the purpose-built blockade runner *Wild Dayrell*, a 320-ton iron side-wheel steamer launched at Liverpool in November 1863, across the Atlantic to Nassau in the Bahamas. On the outbreak of the American Civil War in April 1861, Abraham Lincoln had ordered a blockade by Federal ships of the 3,000-mile coastline of the newly-declared Confederate States; his aim was to prevent the delivery of supplies and weapons from allies both at home and abroad. But Nassau, only five or six hundred miles from the east-coast commercial centres of Savannah, Charleston, and Wilmington, quickly became one of the main hubs for outside trade with the Confederacy. Confederate agents established themselves there and, with the enthusiastic participation of merchants in places like Liverpool, enriched themselves and their associates with contraband trade. Liverpool and Birkenhead shipyards built both blockade runners and ships for the Confederate Navy, as Liverpool merchants shipped in arms and other goods, and returned with cotton for the mills of Lancashire. The *Wild Dayrell* was owned by Edward Lawrence for the Anglo-Confederate Trading Company.

Liverpool was well known for its Confederate sympathies: 'Does anyone... who knows Liverpool doubt that the overwhelming balance of sympathy is on the side of the South?', asked the *Liverpool Albion* in May 1862. On the other hand there is no reason to think that Thomas was demonstrating any personal political stance by agreeing to deliver the *Wild Dayrell*. We have already seen that he witnessed slave auctions, in Brazil and possibly in Nassau too, and that he disapproved of this trade that was so central to the Confederate view of life.

It would appear that his job was simply to deliver the *Wild Dayrell* to Nassau, 'that nest of pirates'; he must have returned to England as a passenger on another ship. However his role would not have been entirely without risk, and it is likely that he was well rewarded. In the event the vessel made just four voyages as a blockade runner from 5th January 1864 on. On her final voyage, in early February, carrying 'a cargo of shoes, blankets, and valuable merchandise', she ran aground while trying to enter Wilmington. Her cargo was successfully discharged by the Confederates, but she was hunted down and finally shelled and set ablaze by a boarding party from the USS *Sassacus*, one of the vessels of the North Atlantic Blockading Squadron.

After this adventure, Thomas returned to the peace of the Isle of Man and his new home. With their move to Rose Hill, the Cubbins would have become part of the Douglas world, rather than that of the Castletown of Thomas's youth or the Liverpool of their early married days. A directory for 1863 describes Douglas at this time as having 12,389 inhabitants, and 'old streets constructed very irregularly, and in many instances ... very crooked and narrow' around the harbour area. However 'handsome terraces and streets have been erected, containing many excellent houses and shops'. Mary was possibly still teaching Esther and Tom at home, or they may have been sent to school for the first time in their wandering young lives.

Once the family had settled at Rose Hill, the younger Cubbin children were all baptised at Kirk Braddan by the Revd William Drury (capable when necessary of preaching in Manx Gaelic), and no doubt also attended Sunday School there. Religious instruction would have formed the backbone of their education, with material as basic as spelling cards supplied by the Society for Promoting Christian Knowledge. By the age of eleven, Tom would have been familiar with such publications as *The Youth's Magazine, or Evangelical Miscellany, The Childen's Friend* and *The Child's Companion*. Child mortality at this time was still horrifi-cally high, and all tended to linger on children's deathbed scenes, and the courage with which their small heroes and heroines passed over into a promised heaven.

As described by his father in *The Wreck of the Serica*, young Tom is a more than conventionally pious child. Not only does he faithfully care for his beloved little brother James, but in the teeth of a hurricane he passes his time reading the Bible and singing hymns. He never complains of hunger or thirst, even though, when they are confined to an open boat after the *Serica* has sunk, his parents can see him visibly wasting away. As the family approach the shores of Madagascar, he reassures his father 'with the greatest composure, "Oh! never mind, Pa, you stop here with us, and we will all go to heaven together"'. He is even singing at the end, 'Teach me to live that I may dread the grave as little as my bed', the words which would eventually be carved on his memorial stone.

It would appear that Thomas Cubbin was able to live for several years at Rose Hill without going to sea at all, for he tells us that 'We had previously made a small competence, and had been living a few years within our income, having all the comforts we wished. But our family having increased very much, we made up our minds to this voyage for their benefit'.

What he does not mention in his *Serica* narrative is that on 19th September 1866 he sailed out of Liverpool as Second Mate of the 2,800-ton emigrant steamer *Helvetia*, en route for Cobh and New York. The *Helvetia* belonged to the National Steam Ship Navigation Company, and her master was Captain William Hyslop Thompson, remarkably only twenty-six years old to Thomas's forty-three. As well as her four mates, boatswain and carpenter, the *Helvetia* carried no fewer than ten stewards, four cooks, forty-five seamen, five engineers and twen-ty firemen, all attired in the company's uniform. The crew agreement warned that stewards would be held responsible for all lost plate and linen, and ordered firmly 'No Grog'.

This voyage to New York and back lasted just a month, for which Thomas was paid eight pounds (three pounds less than the first mate, thirty shillings more than the other two). It would have given him a glimpse of a completely differ-ently style of seafaring from anything he was used to. For the cabin class passengers, at least, the *Helvetia* was extremely luxurious. An account survives, written by one of them who sailed from Liverpool to New York on a similar voyage a year later. When the *Helvetia* called at Cobh, a tug brought on board:

> ...140 [steerage] passengers and several cabin passengers. Accompanying the tug were a bevy of pedlars, some with fruit and some with vegetables etc., and one of them had sets of bog oak jewellery. I bought and several of the passengers bought, and I believe he would have sold all he had, had the tug not rung her bell.
>
> *25th October*, the rolling and pitching of the vessel is very uncomfortable to all, but we are not to grumble. We are on the ocean on the tail end of October. A rough night threatens us, with the wind nearly dead ahead. Roll, roll, clatter, clatter, creak, creak, grumble, grumble...

On 27th October some of the cabin passengers were playing leapfrog with the captain.

> There is a good arrangement for the ladies; an appropriate compartment is set aside for their convenience during stormy weather, and they are provided with every convenience. The stewardess can administer to their wants, and they are in better shape to assist each other. They are excused from sitting at table, take their meals there, and not to be seen if seasick.
>
> *28th October*, I omitted to state yesterday evening, the ladies had a private concert in their stateroom. The captain and lady were there.
>
> *2nd November, nine days at sea*, The steerage passengers are kept quiet by plenty of good victuals and fresh air. They are brought up on deck early in the morning until breakfast is nearly ready for them. They are then permitted to remain but a short time after breakfast below, and are hustled up on deck again ... invariably they are by far the greater part of the time on deck.

Cabin passengers enjoyed games of cards and 'tricks and sports', while drinking champagne and brandy. Divine service was held in the saloon on Sundays.

One ambition still remained unfulfilled for Thomas and Mary Cubbin, ownership of a vessel of their own; the following year would see it happen. In 1863, in Carleton, New Brunswick, a merchant named Henry W. Wilson had had a three-masted wooden barque built, launching her as the *Estelle*. She was sailed across the Atlantic with a cargo of timber, then both ship and cargo were sold in Liverpool. Thomas bought her from her second owner in 1867, changing her name to *Serica*. She was 139ft long and 31ft wide (543 gross tonnage, 503 net, according to her registration, although he tells us she was 'of 560 tons'), and he was immensely proud of her seaworthiness. He writes that she was 'first class ... staunch and strong, and well fitted and found throughout, and what sea-faring men would call a fine sea-boat'. For the first time in his life his name was inscribed on a ship's log as both master and owner.

Although his was a sailing vessel, the cargo he obtained was of coal. It was to be delivered to Aden, that ancient natural harbour at the entrance to the Red Sea which had become an important transit and bunkering port for steamships operating in the Indian Ocean. Thomas's intention was probably then to pick up another cargo and sail onwards to India.

Coal is notoriously dangerous because of the ever-present danger of spontaneous combustion. In *Youth: A Narrative*, Conrad describes the discovery of a fire at sea:

> The first thing I did was to put my head down the square of the midship ventilator. As I lifted the lid a visible breath, something like a thin fog, a puff of faint haze, rose from the opening. The ascending air was hot, and had a heavy, sooty, paraffiny smell. I gave one sniff, and put the lid down gently. It was no use choking myself. The cargo was on fire.

There follows a subtly long-drawn-out and terrifying account of the spontaneous combustion of a cargo of coal, leading to the panicked abandonment of the ship by some at least of her crew.

But fire was only one of many dangers to a nineteenth-century vessel. For today's seamen, protected by all the sophistication of modern technology, it is deeply disturbing to remember how frequently ships were still being lost in those days. In the parlours and taverns of Liverpool there would have been much talk of cargoes delivered and profts made, but at least as much again of vessels wrecked and other disasters at sea.

Thomas would have known of individual tragedies, such as the death of Captain Archibald Lister, who had just set out from Liverpool for China on the barque *Mary Lee* in March 1860 when a heavy sea swept him against the vessel's lee bulwarks. The captain was so badly injured that he died before he could be

There is no known image of the Serica, *but this painting of the barque* Jardine Brothers *by William Howard Yorke, 1880, shows an exactly similar vessel battling a rough sea. Like the* Estelle/Serica, *the* Jardine Brothers *was built in New Brunswick.*

NEW BRUNSWICK MUSEUM, SAINT JOHN, N.B. (1966.28)

The ever-present dangers of life at sea – the Mary Elizabeth, *on which Thomas Cubbin had sailed to Bombay in 1845, was wrecked at Punta Gallinas in northern Colombia four years later.*

ILLUSTRATED LONDON NEWS, SEPTEMBER 22ND 1849

brought into Holyhead for medical attention. Thomas would have heard of the loss of ships like the 783-ton *Volunteer*, which had made record-breaking voyages between Liverpool and Calcutta, but ended her days wrecked on the Cargados Carajos Shoals, north-east of Mauritius, in 1864. Not even a moored ship in a sheltered harbour was safe. The full-rigged *Aladdin* also sailed out of Liverpool in 1864, arriving at Calcutta via Bombay on 15th September. Less than three weeks later a cyclone struck the area, drowning 12,000 people and wrecking 110 vessels in the harbour. The *Aladdin* was so badly damaged as to be a total loss.

Some ships simply disappeared without trace. The *Ganjam* had set out for Liverpool from Akyab in Burma on 8th April 1864 with a cargo of rice. She was last 'spoken' on 8th June at 29°S, 44°E, but never seen again. Disasters could even occur when a vessel was disquietingly close to home. The brig *Elizabeth Buckham* had sailed all the way from Demerara with a cargo of cotton, rum, sugar and coconuts when she entered the Mersey on 26th November 1866. There she sank on the Great Burbo Bank in a Force 10 gale, with the loss of her cargo and all ten crew.

But all this was simply part of the life of the mercantile marine; the risks were high, but the spoils could be worth it. More surprising to the modern mind is the fact that not only did Thomas and Mary Cubbin take their two young sons – James so small as still to be unsteady on his feet – on their maiden voyage in the *Serica*. They also left behind in the Isle of Man their four daughters: Esther would have been twelve by then, but little Mary was only four, Jane two, and Amy Mona scarcely weaned. She had been born just five months before the *Serica* sailed, yet her mother chose to go on a long sea voyage without her. Presumably all four were left at Rose Hill in the care of relatives.

From Thomas's account of Mary first going on board the *Serica* in Birkenhead – with Tom and James and their favourite dog, brought all the way from Rose Hill – it is clear that she is used to making the best of the cramped confines of a sea-borne home: 'During the day my wife was very busy placing our effects to her own liking'. All four of them sleep together in the captain's cabin, with Mary and the two boys confined there during the worst of the ensuing storms.

For eleven-year-old Tom this must all have seemed the most exciting of adventures. A couple of generations later Tessa Karran, a daughter of Castletown's most famous sea-going family, would recall a childhood spent with her two brothers, crossing the world's oceans under sail in their father's ship *Manx King*:

> Few children could have had a happier or more thrilling life. And at sea, no matter how hard a gale might blow, it never interfered with our play. The sailors had made us wooden sleds with wheels as runners and we lay flat on them and pitched when the ship pitched and rolled when she rolled! ... We had become so accustomed to the motions of the ship that we seemed in some way to settle on the deck much after the fashion of the storm birds on the ocean waves and, though in our short lives we must have encountered more storms than have fallen to the lot of most mortals who live on land, not one of us ever suffered even a sprained limb...
>
> By this time my elder brother was growing up ... he knew the name and location of every line and spar on the ship and he could even give all the correct orders for shortening sail or putting the ship on its course. So it was only natural that he should be more with my father and the officers than playing games with my younger brother and myself. We all enjoyed climbing the rigging...

The *Manx King* was a very much larger and more commodious ship than the *Serica*, but young Tom must have anticipated just such excitements. In *The Wreck of the Serica* Thomas gives little indication of how relations stood between his family and the crew before the hurricane; perhaps their experiences were not as happy as those of the Karrans. The *Manx King* was sailed by the same crew journey after journey; the *Serica* sailed from Birkenhead with fourteen men most of whom, as far as we know, had never sailed together before.

In *The Nigger of the Narcissus*, Conrad has his elderly AB Singleton say, 'Ships are all right. It is the men in them!' And not for the first time, Thomas was to have problems with his men during this voyage. The *Serica*'s crew was indeed a motley one, led by a mate, John Cruickshank, who was only twenty-two years old. Cruickshank had been discharged from his previous ship, the Australian Currie Line's *Albert Victor*, in Liverpool a full five months earlier. On board the *Serica* he initially seems, in Thomas's eyes, 'all I could have wished him to be', and he even helps fight off a shark when they have had to abandon the sinking ship. But Thomas will eventually blame Cruickshank for the loss of his sons when they land on Madagascar. A 'splendid swimmer', he is given charge of saving little James, but puts his own skin first.

The second mate was a twenty-eight year old Shetlander, David Nicholson, who had sailed on Isambard Kingdom Brunel's *Great Britain* only a few months before. The carpenter – a vital role – was another twenty-eight year old, Alexander MacKenzie, born in Fife, who had not been to sea for two years. He let Thomas down by damaging the *Serica*'s starboard pump at the height of the storm. The cook was thirty-nine year old Daniel Roberts, from Cowes in the Isle of Wight, who until October had been sailing with the Royal Navy on HMS *Sanspareil*. He too was to behave despicably when the *Serica* was in most danger, inciting the rest of the crew to break into the cabin and demand grog. Thomas calls him 'about the most idle, insolent, and mutinous character I ever knew'.

ABs on the *Serica* included the Orkneyan Andrew Stout, twenty-eight, from Stromness. His cowardly conduct on the shore of Madagascar would earn him Thomas's outburst, 'You mean, contemptible heap of humanity!' Forty-two year old Thomas Hall from Northampton would commit the meanest of thefts when the family were at sea in their open boat. The other ABs were Edward Fennell, twenty-five, born in Hampshire, discharged in November from the *Braganza*; Alexander McKenzie, forty, of Belfast, discharged from the *R. Jones*; another Liverpudlian, twenty-two year old Edward Kiffin, who had come straight from the *Helena* in Greenock; and a Waterford man, Jeremiah Driscoll, discharged from the *Chapultipee* in Leith. The last two members of the crew were Cape Verdeans, Antonio Jenkins, forty-two, and thirty-six year old Joseph Mar — (his full name is indecipherable on the crew list).

Enlisted as an Ordinary Seaman was a seventeen-year-old youth from the Isle of Man, William Edward Clarke, who was on his first voyage. The ship's boy was only a little older than Tom Cubbin, but the fourteen-year-old Liverpudlian Charles Alexander Radcliffe already had tales to tell; he had come to the *Serica* from another Brunel vessel, the huge iron sailing-steamship *Great Eastern*, which the year before had laid the first telegraph cable under the Atlantic.

Thomas Cubbin, nothing if not fatherly at this time of his life, always writes tenderly of these two youngest members of the crew, to whom he and Mary seem to have acted as parents. When they have to abandon the *Serica*, he records that Clarke and Radcliffe are 'crying bitterly, and said that my wife had promised them that they should be with her to the last'.

MADAGASCAR

● **Tamatave**
(Toamasina)

● Andovoranto

● **Antananarivo**

● Mahanoro

● **Mahila**
(Mahela)

Tropic of Capricorn - - - - - - - -

Tom and James Cubbin died at
Mahila Bay (19°29'S, 48°29'E),
eleven days after the sinking of the
Serica. Tom's remains were buried
at Mahila; James's body was never
found. Thomas and Mary Cubbin
then travelled some 260 miles to
reach the island's main port of
Tamatave (modern Toamasina).
From there they undertook another
perilous voyage to Mauritius on
board the bullocker *Caprice*, en
route for England and home.

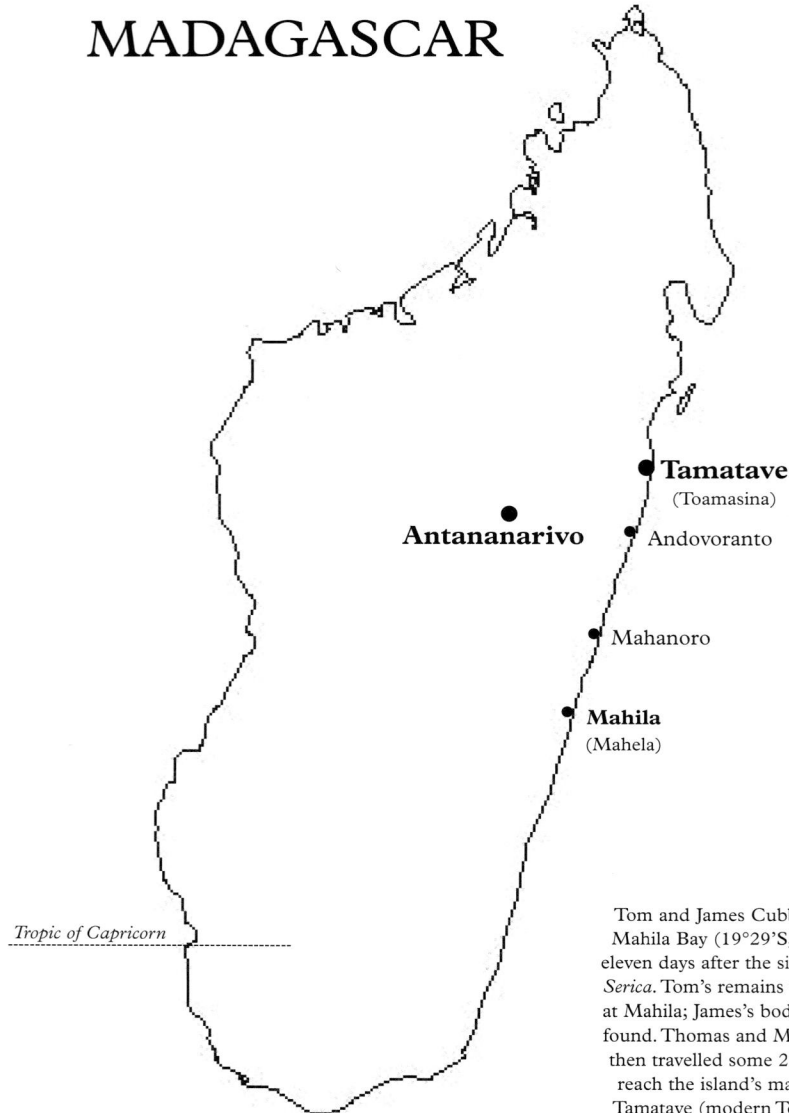

**Names according to Thomas's
text in bold; modern names,
where they differ, in brackets.**

The voyage starts badly when they have to leave Birkenhead on a Sunday, never a thing a seaman with an ounce of superstition – or indeed respect for the Sabbath – in him would choose to do. From then on Thomas's own words cannot be bettered, as in *The Wreck of the Serica* he paints a picture of the most terrifying of storms, the loss of his ship, and the torments that ensue for his family. They are eventually tossed ashore, however, on the shores of an island which may need some explanation.

Madagascar in 1868 was a place which most seafarers had long avoided, a mysterious island of volcanic mountains and fetid swamps, of animals seen nowhere else on earth, and of people whose reaction to strangers could be utterly unpredictable. This is the world's fourth largest island, about the size of France, and possessed of a great variety of dramatic scenery. To follow Thomas and Mary's gruelling overland journey towards home and safety one has first to envisage the hazards of the long, straight coast on which they landed.

Their little boat turns over in the surf at 'Mahila' Bay, about two-thirds of the way down the island's east coast, and they seek help in the nearest village (now known as Mahela or Mahaela), which is only a short distance inland. But this place is the best part of 200 miles south of the chief port of Tamatave, which they have to reach in order to escape from the island, in their wounded and grief-stricken state, and find their way back to England.

The chief characteristic of this coast was, and to a large extent still is, the long chain of waterways which lies just inland. Huge rivers empty into the sea, their mouths clogged with sand, and between them in Thomas's day lay a series of disconnected and seemingly endless lakes and swamps. There were no roads – in any case the wheel had yet to reach the island – and moving from place to place meant travelling in canoes, which had to be lifted and carried over each stretch of land between the waterways. Anyone too important, or too ill, to walk these stretches would be carried by native bearers in a *filanzana*, a sort of flimsy sedan chair or palanquin; this is how Thomas and Mary cover most of the distance between Mahila and Tamatave after their rescue. Almost the whole way they are within hearing, if not within sight, of 'our old enemy', the pounding, roaring surf which has taken the lives of their children.

At a more favourable time of year this coast can be comparatively pleasant.

The Bishop of Mauritius, in an account published in 1864, wrote:

> ...the beach is one mass of rolling surf; above that is sandy but rich soil, running in embankments parallel with the sea, and covered with a great variety of trees, plants, and flowers, amongst which many beautiful kinds of birds are seen and heard. This slip of land, about a mile on the average in width, has again parallel with it a magnificent chain of lakes, which go inland for many miles, and in some of which are large and fruitful islands. Looking at these lakes with one's back to the sea, the timber-covered hills of the centre of the island are very clearly seen, and behind them the blue mountains which form the water-shed of the island. From these mountains innumerable streams run down into the rivers, some of which are very wide and beautiful.

But in the rainy season traversing these endless waterways could be gruelling and, for Europeans, potentially fatal. The Austrian traveller Ida Pfeiffer, who in 1857 narrowly escaped from Madagascar with her life (only to die the following year, probably of malaria contracted there), described one of her journeys:

> The ... lakes which we had to traverse were very small, and so were the rivers. A great loss of time was occasioned by the fact that very few of these silent highways communicated with each other. Between almost every lake and stream and its neighbour lay a little tract of dry land, from a hundred to a thousand paces in length, so that our boats were continually being unloaded and carried over... Our way lay near the sea-coast, and we constantly heard the sound of the breakers...

> In these lower lands and, with few exceptions, along the whole coast of Madagascar the climate is very unhealthy, and dangerous fevers are prevalent. The reason for this probably is that the land lies deep, and the rivers are choked up with sand at their mouths. In the rainy season the water pours unchecked over the plains, forming swamps and morasses, the exhalations from which, in the hot months from November till the end of April, produce a malignant miasma.

But Madagascar had long been a place to avoid for reasons other than the terrain and the weather. While the Cubbins are in Madagascar the island's queen dies, and they are witnesses to native rituals marking the event. Thomas writes, 'Now, since England has a treaty with the country, no Jezebel Queen will dare again to massacre the Christian community with impunity, as before has happened'. He is not referring to the queen who has just died, Rasoherina, but to her aunt, mother-in-law and predecessor, Ranavalona I, who fortunately for him

Queen Ranavalona I of Madagascar (1778–1861), has been dubbed 'the female Caligula' for her extreme cruelty towards her own subjects. She also ordered the death of almost every European landing on her shores. Her niece and daughter-in-law Rasoherina (below) was the queen who died on 1st April 1868, while Thomas and Mary Cubbin were in Madagascar. The royalty and nobility of Madagascar affected elaborate European-style dresses and uniforms at this time.

ILLUSTRATED LONDON NEWS, 19TH NOVEMBER 1881

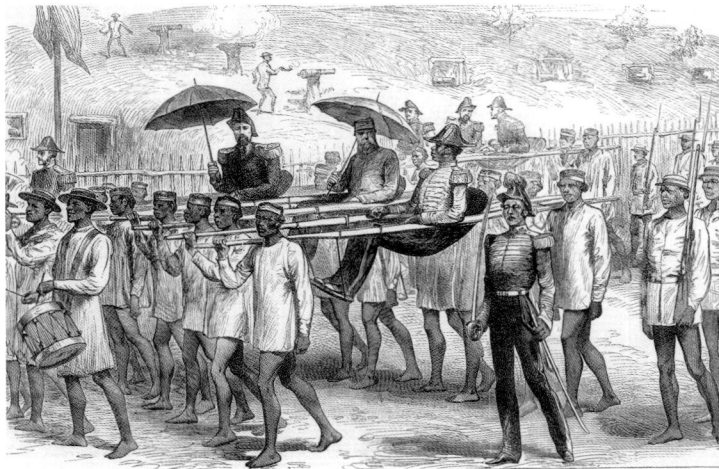

'British naval officers arriving on a visit to the Hova governor of Tamatave'. The wheel was late to reach Madagascar, and people of importance were traditionally carried on a filanzana or palanquin. When they were not in canoes, this was how Thomas and Mary travelled for most of their long trek north to Tamatave.

had been dead since 1861. If Thomas and Mary had been washed up at Mahila seven years earlier, they would have been lucky to get any further than the beach without being killed.

Ranavalona I was one of the great monsters of history, a woman whom a biographer has dubbed 'the female Caligula'. Born a commoner in about 1788, she succeeded by chance in marrying the Merina prince who in due course became Radama I of Madagascar. When he died in 1828 she quickly claimed the throne. There followed more than thirty years of cruelty and bloodshed, during which no European seaman would have dreamed of landing on Madagascar if he could possibly avoid it. Ida Pfeiffer wrote of Ranavalona:

> Her hatred for the British was very great, and extended to every thing that came from England, even to the cattle introduced from that country. All people of English descent were to be killed, or at least banished from her dominions; nor did the French find favour in her eyes. She set her face generally against civilization, and tried hard to stifle its every germ. She drove away the missionaries, prohibited Christianity, and made all communication with Europeans difficult. Her subjects, especially those who did not come from the race of the Hovas, from which she came, she treated with great severity and cruelty: for the smallest offences the most rigorous punishments were inflicted, and sentences of death were, and still are, executed daily.

It was even said that she had a series of human skulls set up along the shores of her island kingdom to discourage European invasion.

Fortunately for Thomas and Mary Cubbin, the crew of the *Serica* and the many other Europeans who would come into the orbit of Madagascar during the latter years of the century, Ranavalona was succeeded, at least for a time, by a son as benevolent as she was evil. Conceived without the help of her husband – indeed born some fourteen months after his death – the young prince Radama managed to keep peace with his mother while fully intending to reverse all her policies as soon as she was dead. The missionary William Ellis described him while he was heir apparent as:

> ...unselfish, generous to a fault, instinctively abhorrent of cruelty and bloodshed, the advocate, the friend, the helper of the poor. To the latter, and to the great body of the people, the existing regime had been strong, oppressive and hopeless, the most destructive of human life which had perhaps ever existed in the country.

Zebu, the native lyre-horned cattle, being driven to Tamatave for export. It was on a 'bullocker'
carrying such cattle that Thomas and Mary made their final storm-tossed escape from Madagascar.

ILLUSTRATED LONDON NEWS, *17TH SEPTEMBER 1864*

Radama II signed treaties with France and England and welcomed Christian missionaries back into Madagascar. Another member of the London Missionary Society, Ebenezer Prout, wrote of him as king:

> It is most remarkable that Radama II should have formed views of policy so large and liberal, so enlightened, humane and patriotic as those which form the foundation of his throne; that the son of such a mother, trained up under a despotism so dark, and restrictive and cruel, should have adopted such principles of religious freedom and political economy, as equal civil liberty and universal free trade principles, which our own nation has been so slow to learn, and which are still repudiated in many lands where civilization is far advanced.

But Radama did not exercise his benign rule for very long, for in May 1863 he mysteriously disappeared. He may have been murdered, or it has been suggested that he escaped and lived to old age in hiding. His wife Rabodo agreed to conditions imposed by his ministers, and was crowned queen with the name Rasoherina. It was she who died on 1st April 1868, six days after Thomas and Mary Cubbin reached Madagascar.

Thomas describes their long trek up the island's coast, helped on their way by native people and by an assortment of missionaries, consular agents and benevolent local traders. He manages to note some of the attractions of the scenery:

> Some of the rivers and banks were beautiful with overhanging trees and plants, and some places flowers. We saw many birds of splendid plumage, and often the beautiful king-fisher in his haunt.

He even recovers something of his old sense of humour when one of the missionaries, the Revd Thomas Campbell, displays his unfamiliarity with the use of a hammock:

> I slung it up for him for the first time. We all had a very hearty laugh at his fruitless efforts to get into it. At length I gave him a lesson in the art; but worse still, he got in on one side and tumbled out at the other. Eventually, I assisted him in.

But from now on, let Thomas speak for himself...

THE HURRICANE WRECK OF THE SHIP

'SERICA'

A

PERSONAL NARRATIVE

OF

PERIL AND ADVENTURE

BY HER CAPTAIN

THOMAS CUBBIN

—— 'To Cry to the Sea That Roared to Us, To Sigh
to the Winds, whose Pity Sighing Back Again
Did us but Loving Wrong'

LONDON

SIMPKIN, MARSHALL & CO., STATIONERS, HALL COURT

LIVERPOOL

EDWARD HOWELL, CHURCH STREET

DOUGLAS

MYLREA & ALLEN

1870

PREFACE

THE FOLLOWING NARRATIVE the writer feels quite satisfied has no merit to recommend it to the reader except that it is entirely a narrative of facts, and shortly before it was commenced had as much idea of making a long voyage in an aerial machine as of ever becoming an author; and although having kept a rough abstract, when asked by many friends to publish an account of our most disastrous voyage, ridiculed the thought of ever committing it to print, and yet the details were too harrowing to recite, and it has been a very hard task to again go through, awakening up the thoughts of our sad loss, privation, and suffering. The writer had navigated those seas where the disaster occurred, in command, for many years successfully, and had perhaps too much assurance of still continuing in success, and not sufficiently remembering that we are the humble creatures of an all-wise Creator, by whose merciful providence we are at all times preserved, and not by our own knowledge and skill.

The ship was first class, 560 tons register, staunch and strong, and well fitted and found throughout, and what sea-faring men would call a fine sea-boat; but the great storm was too much for her. Since the sad termination of the voyage, the writer has avoided meeting his old friends as much as possible, not wishing to give a recitation of the sad catastrophe, yet many whom it was impossible to avoid, have expressed a great desire to see the narrative in print.

The newspaper reports being so meagre, might almost be said to be incorrect, in not giving the proper meaning of the report as it was sent to the government authorities; which cause has been the principal inducement for attempting this description of the whole catastrophe.

Thos. Cubbins, Master

DOUGLAS, MARCH, 1870

PERSONAL NARRATIVE

ON THE 6TH DECEMBER, 1867, my wife and two sons came on board the good ship *Serica*, of which I was master. The ship was loaded and ready for sea, lying in the dock at Birkenhead, and bound for Aden. My wife was not ignorant of a sea-faring life. Our son, being the elder of three, ocean-born, was eleven years old at the time. The youngest with us was nineteen months. During the day my wife was very busy placing our effects to her own liking, and seeing that all was secured and ready for whatever weather we might meet at this season of the year in the channel. We had previously sailed long and successfully together. The ship was well-found, staunch, and strong, and was moderately laden.

We were fully expecting to sail next morning, the 7th, the tide answering about 7 o'clock. Most of the crew were on board during the night; all were astir in good time, and some riggers to assist in getting the vessel away. The wind at the time was a strong breeze from the northward. We hauled ahead into the basin; there the pilot and master of the steam-tug came to us. They wanted us not to proceed. The pilot said the tug that had come for us could not tow us to sea. I said, "Others are going, and we will go also". It was a splendid wind to go down channel, if we were outside the banks. No doubt it was self that troubled these worthies. The master of the tug I suppose thought it would be a hard tow out, and he would not be towing by time. The pilot's thoughts, I suppose, were, that there would be a good deal of sea outside, that would make it unpleasant leaving the ship. I do not know that their united influence stopped our further progress; but there was none of the dock officials to attend us through the locks. Having waited and looked for them a long time in vain, the pilot returned to tell us we were too late for tide, and he would not take the ship; after saying so, he walked away.

I felt very much annoyed, for the next day would be the Sabbath, and I never did like Sunday sailing. I went on shore by the waterman's boat to see the dockmaster, and accused him of this neglect. He talked very large and defiant at first, saying we had not the ship at the buoy in time. I said we had, and long before the time. He insinuated that I had spoken a falsehood. I said he looked as much like a liar as I did, and that I would have no further argument, but would communicate with his superiors, bade him good morning, and returned.

The worthy dockmaster soon followed me to as near the ship as we could get without a boat, apologised for what he had before said, admitting that he saw the ship at buoy in time, but was unable to explain why she was not attended through the locks, but he said it was not too late yet. That would not do, for the pilot and steamtug had cleared off. He also said, if I was going to lodge a complaint, kindly to do so through him; and further, he would make sure that we should be next first ship to go out, and ordered our ship into a position where we must go first. I did not resist this proposition, but consented to be a Sabbath breaker.

Next morning, Sunday, December 8th, the dockmaster, true to his word, started us first, and we were hung outside before either pilot or steam-tug came to us.

The morning was moderate and fine, with variable wind, but before we were two hours out, it became very unsettled, heavy rain and a chopping head sea.

About l0 a.m. the pilot left us outside the Bell Beacon. About 1 p.m. the steam-tug left us. The weather was very gloomy, and no land in sight.

My wife and myself began to reflect, how foolishly we had acted in leaving our comfortable home, and four little ones. We had previously made a small competence, and had been living a few years within our income, having all the comforts we wished. But our family having increased very much, we made up our minds to this voyage for their benefit. But, alas, it turned out a most disastrous one. However, it was too late now to repent. We had fairly started, and there was nothing for us but make the best of it, and strive to get through. We were in all eighteen souls on board, including my wife and two children. With various winds and weather we got clear of the channel on the third day, all well. For two days before we reached Madeira, we had thick, gloomy weather, and were without observations. During the night of the 16th, I was on deck, expecting we were in the vicinity of that island. Our dead reckoning showed our position to be twenty miles to westward of it. At daybreak, on the l7th, the weather cleared a little. I got a glimpse of the land; it was not more than half-a-mile off. "All hands on deck quick!" was the cry. Braced up sharp, and hauled her off. It was blowing hard from the northward at the time, a heavy sea on, and we were on a lee shore, we had a very close shave to clear. We felt our minds very much relieved, and were thankful to the Almighty when we got round Madeira once more. I think this was the greatest alarm my wife ever had during her long experience at sea. And I am firmly of [the] opinion, that had the *Serica* struck there not one soul had been saved, but we were still saved to endure great privation and sufferings. From Madeira we sped on our way, making good progress. We passed to the eastward of the Cape de Verde Islands, crossed the Equator, having experienced the weather usually expected there: baffling winds, squalls, calms, and heavy falls of rain. All went on well. We sighted Martin Vass Rocks, and were on the Tropic of Capricorn on the thirty-eighth day from Liverpool. It is not my intention to tire the reader with all the little incidents that occur on board ship on a voyage to India, except to carry down our dates to the scene of our disasters from the Tropic to the Meridian of the Cape of Good Hope. We had a long and tedious passage; and off that Cape we had a great deal of calms and light baffling winds, more than I ever before experienced in those latitudes. During all the month of February we made very poor progress. We were running down our easting on the parallel of 41 degrees. On the 1st of March, we were only in about 30 degrees of east longitude. On that day it sprung up a strong breeze from the N.E., increasing as it veered to the north, and a strong gale when it got to N.W. It blew hard up to near midnight, when it had veered to west, then suddenly dropped calm, causing the ship to roll fearfully in the heavy sea. The calm continued until the 4th, the ship rolling heavily all that time. On that day a breeze sprung up as before, from N.E., increasing to a gale when it got to north. Next day, the 6th, it blew a heavy gale from the N.W. at sunset, veering to west, and again suddenly dropped calm, the ship again rolling fearfully; I confess I never did experience the same before. The wind most times veering to S.W., at which point it mostly blew hardest, moderating as it drew more south. The calm continued as before, until the 8th, when we got a breeze from the southward, soon increasing to a brisk gale, and inclining to the eastward; by this time we were on the meridian of about 50 degrees east. We steered away to the N.E., for the eastern passages up the Indian sea, fully expecting to make up our easting before we reached the Tropic. The wind increased to a strong gale on the 10th, and the weather very gloomy. On the 11th, we had similar weather, the wind having still scanted, steered for Boscawen passage in order to keep the sea abaft the beam, there being a very heavy sea on at the time. At noon, the weather was very gloomy, the barometer steady, and showing no indication of a storm. Yet I often expressed myself as not understanding the matter. But I determined, as soon as I got within the limit of the trade wind (which is considered 26 degrees south latitude), if there was no improvement in the appearance of the weather, that I would run no further. On that evening we had reached within those limits. During the night, the atmosphere would sometimes break, and a few stars shine out for a moment, and again all would be covered as with a mantle.

March 12th. At 2 a.m. there was no improvement in the weather; yet the barometers were still steady. I decided to run no further, shortened sail, wore ship, and hove-to on the port tack under lower maintopsail. Daylight, wind increasing to a heavy gale, yet the barometers gave no indication of a coming storm. But I determined to prepare; had royal yards and all possible top hamper sent down; had the sails doubly made fast to the spars; extra lashings on the spare spars and boats; double relieving tackles on the rudder head; covered and battened cabin skylights and windows, barricaded front of the poop, and made all about the ship as secure as we possibly could.

During that day I felt sure there was a hurricane passing over Mauritius, and often said so; but thought we were on the southern edge of it, and would escape its destructive rotary force, by having only a steady gale. The barometers were steady throughout the day, at 29.80, which strengthened my opinion, but we did not relax our labours in making our ship ready for the worst that might come. Towards evening, it was blowing a very heavy gale; our good ship was lying-to splendidly; the gale continued during the night, increasing in violence.

March 13th. At day-break, a fearful gust came down upon us; all hands were called to shorten sail. The lower maintopsail was the only sail set. We waited, as we thought, for a lull, and started to clew up, but it was blown to pieces. We got up tarpaulins and hammocks in the mizzen rigging to keep [the] ship's head to wind. The storm was now down upon us in all its fury. I went to see the barometers, they were still steady; but shortly afterwards began to fall rapidly; the two men were lashed at the wheel. I myself, for the first time in my life, was lashed on the poop to prevent myself being washed overboard. By noon, the storm was past all description, being almost as dark as midnight, with a spectral light. The barometer had fallen to 29.00. We had only a small place in the after companion to communicate with the cabin. My wife was there, wishing to speak to me; she asked what I thought of the weather and our prospect of getting through it. I said "There was still hope, but at the same time the ship might founder at any moment, and that her hope and trust should be in God. Go down with the children and pray, and prepare for the worst". She replied, "If our case is so hopeless, you come down with us". I said, "No; if I do that the ship would soon be given up and left to herself. I must remain at my post until the last". Past noon, if possible it blew harder, barometers still falling. I ordered a part of the lee bulwarks to be rammed out, to allow the weight of water to escape off the decks. Our ship was still tight, for I ordered the pumps to be often tried, and found very little water in her. The scene was fearful to look upon. At 4 p.m. my wife was at the companion, she wished to know what the weather was like. I told her I was unable to describe it, she said, "What does it look like?" (forgive the answer) I said, "It looks like the mouth of hell," and told her to attend to her prayers. Those were strong expressions to make use of; but at the very time my wife came up, I was contemplating the scene, and I thought it was a good representation of that place of everlasting torments. The sea looked like great avalanches coming out of the clouds; around was like a boiling cauldron, and sometimes the ship looked as if in a deep vortex. It was not the first or second hurricane the writer had experienced in the vicinity of Mauritius, but all other storms dwindle into insignificance compared to this awful one. If I had been a short time in this sad reverie, I was suddenly roused by some very heavy seas striking the ship, one of them damaged the rudder. The barometer had fallen to 28.60. I had been expecting all day to see the masts go over the side; but still everything held on well aloft. Night was again approaching, the barometers still falling. Another heavy sea had struck the rudder, and bent the iron tiller. I signalled the officers to get the fore-topmast cut away. They went about it, but not in the proper manner, by cutting the rigging, without separating aloft. Signalled again that such would not do; told them, if they so cut, it would most likely fall inboard, and be the loss of the ship; told the mate they must separate the upper from the lower topsail yards, natch the mast above the cap, to save the foremast head, and then cut the rigging. He soon returned to say that no man would lay aloft. At that time the iron tiller carried away short off by the rudder head. I then ordered the foremast to be cut away, feeling sure that if the ship fell off into the trough of the sea, she must soon founder. The wind was veering to eastward at the time.

The foremast was cut away; the main and mizen soon followed. By this time it was getting dark. We cut and got the wreck away from the ship as quickly as possible, and then got to the pumps, often up to our necks at them, yet kept them going. The storm continued all night, with very little abatement, the ship (if I might call her that name then) laid well along.

March 14th. At daylight, the wind had veered to the N.E. The scene, our ship a miserable derelict, the sea breaching heavily over her, our best boat was smashed to pieces by the falling of the mainmast, our next best had her stem knocked out by the sea, and her gunwales badly broken in the lashings, the smallest, a double end boat, was split open at both ends, through the sea striking and crushing her in the lashing. The rudders and tillers, etc., of both boats, were washed away. At noon, the wind was north and moderating, and a heavy cross sea on. We kept the pumps going, allowing the men to get something to eat, only two at one time. I ordered the mate to give the crew grog as often as he thought it would do them good. We got the wreck that was about the decks overboard, except such as might be useful in constructing a raft was securely lashed. The crew wanted to sound, and find out what water was in her. I would not allow it. I ordered them plenty of the best fare in the ship, and that they must work away. The only place my poor wife and children could find to keep themselves dry, was sitting holding on in our bed. During the afternoon I was below for a few minutes, standing with my head resting on the bed. The cook had come down for stores. After he had got all he required, I overheard him say to the young steward, "Now I must have some bottles of grog". The young man said, "I dare not give it, the Captain would not allow it". "What," he replied, "there is no Captain now; we are all equal". At these words, I confronted him, and asked who had sent him for the grog? He said, "the crew". I said, "I do not believe you; but if it even is so that they have sent you, go back and tell them that the ship is still under command, and that I am, and will be Master as long as she floats; and if you ever dare to put your foot in this place again, without my permission, I will punish you, even though we should all go into eternity an hour after".

Our only way into the cabin was by the aft companion, the front of the poop being barricaded to resist the sea striking it. The cabin leaked very much, and took the two boys baling out to prevent the water getting down the store room hatch. By the evening the crew were very much exhausted and complaining. I arranged that during the night we would set watches, one watch resting and relieving every two hours.

March 15th. At 2 a.m. I fancied the ship was settling down, and determined on more active measures. Had all hands on deck again at the pumps. Afterwards, taking two with myself, we began getting everything of any weight overboard. We threw over the anchors from the forecastle; part of the cables that was in the fore-hold we let run overboard, and everything heavy, until we got at the coals. Then we divided, one half pumping, the other throwing cargo overboard. I was working the fore-hold, when, during the forenoon, the cry rang through the ship, "Sail ho!' I went on deck, and there was a vessel steering right down upon us; all hands were rejoiced at the sight, and dropped the pumps. I sent them back, saying they must pump away, for if even the vessel did come to our assistance, they might think there was too much sea on to put out a boat, and would only lay by us until it went down. I enquired what the time was, and found it was half an hour to noon. Then taking the bearing of the vessel, said he must see us when he takes his meridian altitude at noon, for we bore due north from him, right in the sun blade. We got our ensign, union down, elevated on a ladder, and another signal to a pole, one lashed to the stump of the main and mizen masts. The wind at that time had veered to W.S.W., and was moderating. The vessel came on under easy sail, until we got glimpses of her hull, when she trimmed sail, and hauled off to the eastward for a few miles, and then bore off again, we all made sure they saw us. It they did, may God forgive them for their cruel conduct. This was an awful blow to my poor wife, she had got the children and herself ready to leave our ill-fated ship. My only hope now was to keep her afloat. We all went to work again, throwing cargo overboard and keeping the pumps going. I overheard the cook inciting the men at the pumps to break into the cabin and help themselves to the drinkables. I called him to account for his insubordinate talk, and was on the point of chastising him for it, and with difficulty I restrained myself from so doing, ordered him to the pumps, and told him if he used such talk again, or left the pumps till he was relieved, his body should suffer for it. This cook was about the most idle, insolent, and mutinous character I ever knew. He professed being an infidel, and not caring for death. If he did show neglect, after this caution, he took care not to let me find him away from his post. Towards evening, the crew were complaining of the work, and said they could not keep at it. I said, "What do you mean? You are not working for me; everyone is working for his life; and I am working as hard as any of you". The crew no doubt were fatigued; I was very much so myself; yet I think the cook's evil counsels had a very bad effect; he was indeed a bad man. My wife by this time had informed me, that he somehow got into the cabin during the height of the storm, and was then asking the young steward to give him some grog, which she overheard, and spoke to him about. He said he might as well have some, it would be his last, for we might all go to the bottom any minute. She said, he should not have it. I think it was well for us all that my wife was there, else I believe he would have helped himself, and during my absence working in other parts of the ship, others of the crew might have done the same, and perhaps all been lost. My chief mate and some of the crew worked well. The mate up to this time was all I could have wished him to be. During the afternoon, the carpenter was overhauling the starboard pump. He was stupidly driving the lower box down with the iron break in my absence. I once saw him do so before, but stopped it, and made him get a handspike, and told him never to use the break for that purpose again. Yet he had done so on that occasion with fatal effect, knocking a hole in the chamber of the pump.

As soon as I knew of this to us sad accident, I got a derrick rigged, and hove the pump up, secured the hole with white lead, canvas and sheet lead over. When we lowered again, we could not get the pump tail into the well after trying all possible means. A good deal of water got down through the pump hole during the operation, darkness came on us, and we had to secure it for the night to keep out water; intending by the morning light to have it up again, and cut the end off, where it would not enter the well.

Through this sad disaster, we were able to work only one pump during the night.

March 16th. Long before daylight, I had all hands out again, leaving one watch at the pumps; commenced with the rest getting up stores and provisions by the after companion, to clear away to get at the cargo. Threw all overboard as we got it up. Before daylight, we were working out the cargo from the after-hold. I was working in the hold, in the after-run. There was very little cargo right aft, and the water was making a great noise there. My gang wanted very much to work under the break of the store room deck, to find out what depth of water was there, but I would not allow it. The crew were murmuring, and slipping away when a chance offered. My wife and son were assisting at the cargo with them, and reported. When some went away, I went and got them back again.

At 8 a.m. fear began to take possession of their hearts, that the ship would suddenly sink, and take all down with her. I expostulated with them, and said the ship was our only chance of saving our lives, and that it would require good boats to live in the sea that was on then; besides, the weather looked wild, and our boats that were left were shattered and broken in the storm. I got them to work again, and while down had a little water passed up into the cabin. In a very short time they broke again, and their cry was, "She will founder and take all hands with her". I strove to cheer them, saying, "We had over two months' water on board, and plenty of provisions; let us only keep the ship afloat, and we will be all right". But it was all to no purpose, for by this time fear had taken full possession of them. Finding that the hold was clear of gas, the last thing I did before I came up out of it, was to go round with a light and examine the ship's upper works, and in the way of the channels, expecting to find her very much strained and opened; but it was not so, she was tight in all her upperworks, to my great astonishment. I then felt sure that the damage must be in her bottom, through falling on the wreck of her spars, during the storm, before we got clear of it.

Up to this time my wife had confidence in my opinion, that the ship might be kept afloat, and was urging on the crew to get the cargo overboard, and also helping herself; but during my absence below examining the ship, the chief mate having fallen into the same fears as the crew, distressed her by telling her that the ship might founder any minute with all on board, and advised her to prevail on me to abandon the ship.

When I got on deck again, all on board were clamouring to leave her; but I would not yield, and ordered them to get the hose of the deck pump down the forward ventilator, and work that until we got the starboard main pump cut and placed. It was to no purpose, they refused to do so. I told them there was very little hope of our lives being saved by the boats; that the nearest land, the islands of Mauritius and Bourbon, were at least two hundred and fifty miles off, bearing north. But still they were determined to abandon the ship, by taking to the boats. I then ordered the carpenter to repair the boat on the fore deck house that had her stern knocked out, and otherwise damaged, telling the crew at the same time that there would be very little chance of saving our lives by the boats; and ordered and showed them how to construct a raft that would answer as a floating breakwater to hang the boats to. I then told them above all things they must get some water from below; not one would go in the hold for it.

I took two or three men with myself to get the small boat off the skids on to the poop to repair her, which I did in a very rude manner, for it would have taken a long time to do her properly. I told my wife to get the children and herself ready to go in the boat. When finished, we got her in the davits, put a small breaker with some water in her, two bags of bread, and three or four cheeses. I then got my poor wife and children in her, I kissed them, thinking it might be the last time. They wished me to be in the boat with them. I said no, I must be the last to abandon the ship. We lowered, and got the boat safely afloat, the chief mate and Hall, A.B., being in her to attend the tackles. It was intended that the mate should come up out of the boat again, that she should hang astern, and Hall attend her. From what they afterwards said, she would not hang astern, and they cut her adrift, and kept her with the oars.

After the small boat was afloat, I went to get the raft completed. At this time our infidel cook was as much afraid of his life as any other on board. He went to the pumps, and said he would pump until he dropped, before-time he had to be driven to them. About noon, the raft was completed, and got it successfully launched; a good rope was attached to it, which I ordered should be kept on the top ready at any time to cut; it was passed astern with one man on it.

The carpenter by that time had finished the other boat, and we got her safely launched. I told them again that it was most necessary that they should get some water from below, but none of them would go down for it.

I then told them, there was plenty of preserved provisions and stores in the cabin and store-room; that they might go down and help themselves to everything except wines and spirits. Two men were minding the boat, and the rest went down and got what they pleased. I reminded them again that they should get up water. They began to disagree about which ought to go. Some of them commenced crying, saying "the ship would go down before they got away from her". This was indeed a trying scene. I ordered them into their boats. Andrew Stout got down and found a lot of cutlasses and bottles of grog, which he very properly threw overboard. The rest of them soon followed him into the boat. Radcliffe and Clarke were crying bitterly, and said my wife had promised them they should be with her to the last; I said, "So you shall, but for the present, get into the boat". When they were all in, they said they would not go without me. I told them to go to the raft, naming two or three that should come back to me with the boat, and leave all the rest of them on the raft, intending when the boat came back, to get some water up. Again they said they would not go without me; when I told them, if they would not obey my orders, I would have nothing more to do with them. They then went, and I passed their raft-rope and made it first right aft on the ship.

As soon as they got to the raft, and some upon it, they began shouting and screaming for me to let them go. I said, "I would not; when it is requisite, you can cut the raft-rope"; they replied, "No, it is foul under the raft, and the ship will go down, and take us with her". They screamed again, and I let them go. I called them in the boat to come to the ship, but they would not. Except my dog, I was then alone on board the doomed ship. I went down and looked at the barometers, although this was the third day from the storm, the reading was only 28.95, and the weather looked squally. I got up as high as I could and looked around, hoping there might be some friendly sail in sight; but alas, there was no such succour near.

I was then utterly hopeless, and knew not what further to do, I did not think the boats could live many hours. I knelt down and prayed Almighty God to guide and assist me, and surely He heard my prayers; for I rose up refreshed, and felt again a ray of hope; and the first time for many days I felt anhungered. I went forward and found a kettle of hot coffee that had been prepared for the crew, who in the hurry had left without using it. I got a mug of it, and waded aft again, got some bread, and made a hearty meal, it being the first food I had eaten for some time. My wife by that time was very anxious I should leave the sinking ship, she and the children had been calling a long time, to which I fear I paid very little attention. I then told them, I would soon be with them; went down into the cabin, and picked up a few things the sailors had left strewed about, a few bottles of port wine, two or three tins of sardines, two or three tins of preserved meats, and one jar of jelly. I sent these afloat in a case for them to pick up. The boat looked so deep, that I dare not send anything heavy. She was indeed a very poor boat to stand any bad weather. The other boat was double as capable for it, and much larger. I looked at her low gunwales, and only sent a few light things that might be useful; a chronometer and a box with the ship papers, a compass, nautical almanac, and sextant. All these things we might have left behind, for all the good we had of them.

I went round to take a last look at our doomed ship, and see that the pigs, sheep and every living thing was let loose. The water in the ship made her race ahead, the boat and the raft being out of sight of the small boat astern. I had then been about two hours alone on the ship, and the time must have been about 3 p.m., when remembering my wife's promise to the two boys, Radcliffe and Clarke, took a bearing of the raft and other boat, and left the ship. The dog was ready to leap into the boat with me, and very sorry I was to have to beat him back. I got in and we pulled for the raft.

I thought then as we were leaving the ill-fated ship, and think so still, that had we all used our utmost exertions, we might have kept our ship afloat until we were picked up, or rigged jury masts and temporary rudder, and got to Mauritius.

I omitted previously to state that our rudder was washed away in spite of all our efforts to secure it. I thought then what a pity the old system of carrying rudder-pennants was neglected. I have been in ships that had them, and never saw them used or required, but in this instance, I believe that if there had been good pennants on our rudder, we might have saved it and the ship. These reflections were of no use at that time; we had taken to our frail boats, and must make the best of them.

We got up to the raft. The other boat was hanging to it, I called to the boys that they might jump on our oars. We could go no nearer, fearing our boat might be stoved. We got them in. We threw over a bag of bread, so that the other boat might pick it up; and we threw them about half the cheeses. Andrew Stout asked me if I would have another hand? I counted, and found that would make nine persons to each boat. I told him if he came he must jump like the others. He did so. We left the second mate and eight men with the raft and the other boat. He had previously been informed of our position, distance and bearing. I said, "I must now go back to see the last of the ship". The compass we soon threw overboard finding it was useless.

We had some squalls during the evening, but not severe, yet our boat shipped a good deal of water getting back to the ship; she also leaked a great deal, keeping one almost constantly baling out. We got back to the ship about 5 p.m. Our boat did look a miserable craft to be adrift with in the Indian Ocean, the nearest land being at least two hundred and fifty miles off. She only had about nine or ten inches clear side amidships. While under lee of the ship, I said, "We must do something to try and make her more safe". I thought that if we had some canvas, we might with some stanchions get it round her; and if someone would not swim to the ship for it, I would myself do so, for the ship was lurching heavily, and it would have been very dangerous to bring the boat nearer. The mate volunteered to go, and went, and got these articles; he threw them to us, and then swam back again. I nailed some small stanchions on the gunwale, split the canvas, and put a half cloth round. I got one side finished before dark; and although there was neither strength or substance in the construction, it gave the boat [a] so much greater look of safety and comfort, that I longed to get the other side done. Up to midnight it was squally, but we kept our boat under lee of the wreck, which served as a floating breakwater. The poor dog was very anxious to come to us in the boat, but we chided him back.

March 17th, 1868. At 3 p.m., or thereabout, the sheep and pigs made a great noise, the dog barked furiously, the doomed ship made a final plunge, and went down head foremost. As soon as she disappeared, I told them to give way on their oars, the dog would be after us. We pulled hard about one hour, when I told them to ease, I had scarcely spoken, when I saw something coming up astern, thought at first it was a large shark. But no! on nearer approach, we found it was the dog. Gave way again, but it was to no purpose, the dog was close after us. I told them to stop, and when he came alongside to kill him while my sons were asleep (the dog we had brought from home with us, and he was a great favourite with our little boys), it would have distressed them very much to have seen him put to death. My wife said, "Oh! take him in the boat". I said, "He must not come in the boat, he would be the weight of another person, and all the water we had would have been none too much for him alone, he being a very large dog". My wife agreed to his immediate death, when I told her he might follow us most of the day, and shut her eyes. If Miss Burdett Coutts had been there, I think she would also have agreed, seeing the necessity. As soon as he came up one of the men killed him. I could not myself look on, but shut my eyes until it was over, and heard them say, "He has sunk".

About the time the ship went down, the wind lulled to a calm, as if satisfied with its work of destruction, having brought our ship down from a fine, smart looking craft, to an abandoned derelict, and finally sending her to the bottom; at the same time confirming me in my opinion, that with exertion, we might have kept her afloat.

All these thoughts were of no use now. The ship was gone, and all we had to depend on was our little boat. I at once determined to steer for Bourbon, it being a little nearer than Mauritius; so we pulled in that direction. At daybreak, the morning was fine, with heavy cloud-banks round the horizon; when daylight came, we were able to see each other, my wife was in a most deplorable state. Through exposure to the sun and spray the day before, her poor face was scorched and swollen to twice its natural size; all over, it was a mass of tumourous blister; it was indeed painful to look upon. Our little boy, James, when he woke up, stared at her in amazement, and I do not think he knew it was his Ma, until she spoke to him. His own dear face was badly scorched; but I never imagined that the sun would distort any creature's face as hers was. She told me during the night that her face was very painful, but I did not think it was any more than ordinary sun burning, especially as she had been so much in the tropics. Her condition was indeed no enviable one. All the clothes she had on soaked with salt water; her face in this awful state; her position in a small open boat, adrift in mid-ocean; her poor children cramped up in misery, was enough to make many of her sex wish themselves out of the world. She is only a delicate creature to look upon, and at first I feared her committing self-destruction, to get out of her miserable existence; but after the second day and night, although she suffered so much, I found her good spirit had not forsaken her; and I firmly believe she had more courage than any one of the boat's crew.

Soon after daylight, we knelt down, and thanked God Almighty for our preservation so far, and invoking His divine assistance in our further efforts, not omitting to make mention of those in the other boat in our prayers, which we offered up three times a day.

Afterwards, I finished the canvas round the boat, and although very fragile, she appeared very much increased in size.

Before noon, we had a light breeze from S.S.E. Cut one oar to make a mast. We set the only blanket we had taken with us for a sail, and afterwards added the ensign to it, the wind being very light. About 9 a.m. we had breakfast, some biscuit and cheese and half a gill of water each; at about 2 p.m. we had dinner, being a repetition of breakfast, and half a glass of wine each.

During the afternoon I got my poor wife's outer garments hung up and partly dried, and I got the boat put into a little order, throwing overboard the wettest of the bread, and trying to secure a little of it dry. The boat was leaking very much, made efforts to stop the leaks, which was only partially accomplished, it was wonderful how little interest the crew took in keeping the boat afloat or in order; they all seemed in a state of apathy. Before dark we had our frugal fare, again indulging in half a glass of wine each. My poor wife's lips were so sore, that she could put no food into her mouth. On this occasion it was mutually agreed that she should have double allowance of wine. Her position was miserable in the extreme. During the night she placed herself, half sitting, half lying, in the stern-sheets, where, from the leaking of the boat and baling out, her clothes were soon saturated.

At nightfall, we set watches. The mate and Stout were one watch, Hall and myself the other. The boys, Radcliffe and Clarke, kept watch, baling out. Before midnight, it fell calm, we had taken in our sails, and Hall and myself were rowing, when the sky had such a beautiful appearance, which I could not describe. I was gazing on the lovely scene, when my wife, who, I think, had been dozing, started up in great alarm, called out, "Where am I?" and gazed on the lovely appearance of the sky, and talked very strangely. I went aft to soothe her, fearing she would go over the side to get out of her misery. It was some time before I could bring her wandering mind to realise where we were. She sat admiring the lovely scene. It was not a glimpse, it remained two or three hours. I thought [to] myself, can it be a delusion? But no, it was there turn how I pleased. I closed my eyes many times, expecting all would vanish, but when I looked again, it was the same, it was a scene which my wife and I shall never forget. We were steering by the Southern Cross at the time.

As soon as my wife realised her position, she asked for the children, I said they were asleep. Yes, there the poor boys were sleeping, coiled in the bow of the boat, as soundly as if on a bed of down. She said she would like Tom, our eldest son, to witness the beautiful sight; but I thought it a pity to disturb them.

March 18th. Before daylight, we got a light breeze again, which we now thought would be a steady trade wind. We set our sails, and went along very nicely.

At sunrise it was a very fine morning, and a moderate trade wind. Our children woke up after a night of sound sleep, it seemed a blessing to those that could sleep away some of the tedious hours. I did sometimes envy the crew, for they could sleep even with the water washing round and over them, and the two boys, Radcliffe and Clarke, it was impossible to keep awake; even in their watch, baling out the water, they would drop down asleep as if under the influence of narcotic. Sleep seemed to have forsaken my poor wife and myself during the time we were in the boat. My wife had the presence of mind to take an umbrella with her when she left the ship. The first day she could not put it up, the wind being too strong, and the commotion too great, when she got so awfully scorched. The next day she had to hold it up all day, which fatigued her very much in the weak state she was in. But on this, the third day, I fixed it up so that she could sit under [it] without holding it, which was a great relief; but her face was indeed very painful. She often told me that she was sure it must be erysipelas; indeed it was bad enough to call it anything she pleased.

We had a brisk breeze during the afternoon, and made good progress until near midnight, when it became cloudy, and the stars were obscured, and a confused sea. We could then make no progress for want of the stars to steer by. This lasted about two hours. When it cleared a little again we got a glimpse of the stars, and were able to steer.

March 19th. The morning was cloudy, the wind south-easterly, and not steady. During the lulls we helped her along with an oar. So far, our little ones were as well as we could expect, on their short allowance, and cramped position. The little boy, James, was a great deal of trouble, either his Ma had to hold him, or his elder brother, who took turns with her all the time, to keep him in the boat. His little face was very much sunburnt. Our only comfort was at that time, they slept soundly all night in the bow of the boat, without bed, pillow or cushion, as if they had been in a luxurious apartment, although many a spray came on them as they slept. The boat sometimes shipped a little water, enough to spoil all our little stock of provisions.

The chronometer served to show the time, until this day it began to get deranged, through having so many salt water baths to endure. Noon we had clearer weather and a better breeze, and we made fair progress. My wife had great hopes of sighting a vessel, and often told the boys to look out, promising the first that saw her a handsome present. I was glad she had such hope, but did not share it with her. My hope was in making land. The evening was cloudy, and wind moderate; the night was fine but cloudy, which interfered a little with our steering.

March 20th. At daybreak, was cloudy, and moderate weather. Our dear little ones had slept as before. My dear wife very much fatigued, yet having good courage. The stern sheets was her place at night, sometimes she sat up on the thwart for rest, but before she got up I had mostly to wring the water out of her clothes, and though she was suffering very much with her face, we could not spare her a drop of fresh water to bathe it, she scarcely got enough to moisten her throat. The only thing she got was the day before. We opened our tin of sardines, served out the fish, and let her have the oil for her face; she used it once, and laid it by for further use; but the spray coming over, some salt water got in and spoiled it.

We made good progress until sunset, when I thought we could not be more than thirty miles from Bourbon.

After sunset, the weather became very unsettled, and we had a very confused heavy sea. All that we had to bridle with was two oars; it was too light to hang her. We then tried the blanket, set a lug, but she made bad weather with it; I then decided we would keep her fair bow with the oars, which we did all night. It was hard work, for the sea got much worse before midnight. I believe currents also affected us very much in making the sea so confused.

Our dear little ones slept well all night; even though they had many a heavy spray over them, it did not disturb their slumbers. It was a very anxious night for me, for, even though the risk was so great, the men would fall asleep on their oars, and I had to watch them the whole time, even when pulling myself. We looked very anxiously for the daybreak. Our canvas construction was very much damaged by the sea striking it.

March 21st. The much-wished-for daylight at length came. We got up our mast, set the blanket, and let her run to the northward. The morning was very gloomy, and very heavy cloud-banks hung all round the leeward horizon. We ran before a strong breeze, until about 11 a.m. No land was in sight. The wind had then hauled to the eastward, bringing a heavy sea on our beam, which made it very dangerous to keep the boat to.

I said it would not do – we must keep her before the wind, and run for Madagascar, at the same time keeping her away. This announcement caused a great murmur, my poor wife herself joining in it; indeed I felt it a very hard task to express the words, for we were then amongst the drift-wood, sugar-cane and other chips, with plenty of land birds about us, so that we could not be far from the island. The murmuring ran very high, saying they could not live. I said, "Look here, perhaps none of us will live to get to the coast, but I will not rashly run into destruction. My idea is to live as long as we can, and when our time is come, to die like men – to keep the boat to the north-ward five minutes longer, would most likely swamp her. Madagascar is our only chance". "How far is it off?" they said. My reply was, that I had neither book nor chart to refer to, but that it must be over two hundred miles, I was sure; but I thought we might reach it, the trade wind reaching right on to the coast. I knew at the time the distance was much greater.

During the afternoon the wind increased, and before dark the sea was so heavy that it was dangerous to run. I said, "We must keep her fair bow for safety". My crew said, "We cannot". I said, "We must try". My wife's courage was severely tried, but she had still hope, and my ocean-born looked with confidence in my face – it did me good. I said, "Stand by your oars", watched a chance between the seas, and got her round. We had very hard work that night. She shipped one sea that almost half-filled her. It was well we had a bucket and tin to get the water out.

The reader may imagine what sea was on. The steer oar was peaked with its butt under the after-thwart. She put the blade under at that elevation, and broke it short off by the stern, long before midnight. It was so bad that we were often pitched from the oars. They talked about giving it up. Hall said he would do no more. I said, "We will not give it up yet; the most noble death we can die is working for life. Stand by. We'll get her round again, and pull away from the sea". I went aft to help her round. Hall was sitting there, my wife talking to him about his cowardice, and urging him to go to work again. He said, "It is no use – there is no hope for us". I told him to get to the oars. The words, perhaps, were not said in a very amiable manner, but in such a way that he thought it best to obey quickly. We got her round again before it, and as the sea topped, we pulled away with our might from it. There was no sleeping in the boat that night. My wife and little ones were in the stern-sheets. I said, "Mary, I fear we shall not live to see the morning light", in a low tone, that the crew should not hear; "but still hope and pray". My dear boy said, with the greatest composure, "Oh! never mind, Pa, you stop here with us, and we will all go to heaven together".

We pulled before the sea two or three hours, when it seemed not to break so much; got our mast up again, and the blanket on her, which was a great relief, for we were much fatigued.

March 22nd. We were exceedingly glad to see the daylight once more, and we did not omit thanking the Almighty for it. Although the morning was gloomy, and the sea still running heavy, the weather was moderating.

Breakfast once more, but had nothing very tempting, for everything in the boat was perfectly soaked with salt water. I felt sure that there was not a dry stitch in her. We had to eke out the little water that was left, serving twice a day half the quantity we had used before. Out of my share I wetted my lips and left it for the little boy. We indulged in a little wine each at this meal, but very sparingly.

Noon, the weather was fine, the sun shone brightly, and the sea was going down. During the afternoon, I got my wife's outer garments hung up and dried; and got all sail on her, that was both blanket and ensign. During the night, we had the weather cloudy and fine, the stars shone sufficiently for us to steer pretty well.

March 23rd. The morning was fine and clear; our dear little boys slept until long after daylight, no doubt through not having any sleep the night before. Served out the water for the day, the share of my poor wife, two children, and myself, being much less than a quart, the rest were served each in proportion. The want of water was an awful want in the now excessive heat, more especially to our little boy, for he could not get enough at once to quench his thirst, and did not understand why he should only get a spoonful at a time. Our eldest boy bore his privation bravely, never once complaining of either hunger or thirst, yet we could see him as if wasting away.

He passed his time mostly reading the Bible, and singing hymns, when not having the charge of his little brother.

During the afternoon my crew were murmuring very much, and would not believe that I knew where the boat was, or where we were steering to. I explained to them that the course we were going would surely take us on the coast of Madagascar, but that it might be further off than I first named, but, eventually, if we went on, we must strike it. All I could explain did not convince them, and they were talking about giving up. Hall said he would. I felt annoyed, got up, and said, "Look here, I am not at all sanguine that we shall reach the coast; but, as long as I have life, I shall hope, and as long as I have the least hope, I shall work; and any one that will not do the same, I expect them to lighten the boat by giving up our company, and when you are all done and gone, my wife and myself will try". She said, "We will". I think I must have looked very angry, for it had the effect of stopping their murmurs for that time.

I fished the broken oar during the afternoon, so that it would do to steer with, mended the canvas bulwarks that had been knocked adrift, and put the boat in order.

During the night, the wind at times fell very light; at such times we helped her along with an oar. The mate and Hall were changing at it, and not having the bridle fast they stupidly lost it overboard. This was to us a great loss, we turned back to look for it, but did not succeed in finding it.

March 24th. About 3 a.m. the mate was steering. I was laid on a thwart, resting my head. I felt something striking the boat very hard. I inquired what it was. The mate said it was a great shark. I said, "Make him shift, or he will stove the boat's bottom; and look out that he does not break your steer oar". The mate said, "How can I do it?" Hall at the same time said, "It is no use, he will never leave until he gets some of us to eat". I said, "I will give him a broad hint that I have no wish that he should make a meal out of me". His way of action, was dropping astern about thirty yards, then coming full speed, striking the boat under the stern, and rushing up alongside with his great jaws above the boat's gunwale. I got the loose thwart and placed myself in a position to astonish him. The mate let me know when he was coming, and as he came alongside, I made the timber ring on his big head; and he took the hint, so far as not to strike the boat any more. It was then my turn to steer. I had scarcely got hold of the oar, when I felt Mr Shark at the point of it, and I gave him so severe a poke, that, with this second hint, he declined our further acquaintance, and we were not the least grieved at losing such company.

Our children slept soundly until this time, when the little boy, James, commend crying for water. There was a little reserved to wet his mouth, but it did not satisfy.

Soon after daylight we served out the water, about two wine glasses each, my allowance was for the little boy. The morning was fine, and very hot. There was a great many deep-sea fish about us, Bonita, and other descriptions. I made a rude fish-hook out of a nail, but caught no fish.

We had a little wine left and at noon we took half a glass each, our eldest son, up to this time, would not taste. At this time I forced him to take it. This afternoon, I commenced to drench myself with salt water, throwing a bucket over my head, advising the others to do the same, which, after a short time, they did.

About sunset, the weather became very cloudy, which increased as night set in. We prepared for catching rain, which we fully expected, and prayed for; but our prayers were not answered as we desired. No doubt it was for the best; for, had it come, it might have been with a squall, which would perhaps have been fatal to us. In a few hours, the clouds cleared away. We got a glimpse of the stars, which enabled us to steer our course again, pulling with the oars. By midnight we had a light breeze, and set our sails again.

March 25th. Commenced with a light trade wind and passing clouds, using one oar to help her along. Our children rested very badly during the night, the little boy often waking and crying for water. Long before daylight he was crying bitterly, and the crew were murmuring, saying all hope was gone; when our eldest son said, "There was good hope, he had such a beautiful dream: that we were picked up by a large and splendid ship, with a great number of passengers on board. We had got on board and all our troubles ended". At daybreak I told my wife I would open the little jar of jelly, and give the little boy a taste of it, for he was crying very much. This was the only thing we had reserved as a last resource for him. Imagine my surprise – it was nowhere to be found.

I knew it was there the night before, even at midnight. I felt as if struck dumb for a time. My wife had to speak more than once before she got an answer. At length I had to confess I could not find it. This was an awful blow to my wife, losing the only thing we had for the poor little boy. She said, "Now, my child will soon die". I got up with the intention of searching for it.

I soon learned where it had gone. The mate and Stout at once accused Hall of the theft; while he was aft steering, they saw him, while my head was laid down, eat the contents, and throw the jar overboard. At daylight he was lying in the fore put of the boat, saying he could pull no more. When I heard this account of the jelly, I was exceedingly annoyed, and told them there was nothing more for them now to steal. I appealed to them all, that everything we had was served share and share alike, which they admitted. I ordered him to the oar, saying he must do his share of the work as long as he could move; and if he made the slightest murmur, he might dread the result. He obeyed, and attended to his orders. After that I had a severe task to perform, it was to drain the water breaker. The result I knew would have a sad effect upon all; but it had to be done. We got one-and-a-half pints of muddy water out, and served it out. I served Hall the same as myself, with not any. We took to the drenching operation, throwing sea water over us, keeping ourselves constantly wet from head to foot, my wife and the children were treated the same; this kept the body cool. We sometimes washed out our mouths with the water, but with caution not to swallow any. Drenching, and all the operations we could invent, had no salutary effect on our dear little boy, his constant cry was for water. He had to be held and watched the whole time, to prevent him from drinking sea water that was in the boat's bottom. This was a very hot day; the wind being light, we kept one oar going all day. Our boat still leaked a great deal.

During the afternoon I managed to construct a temporary rudder of the boat's loose thwart, so that we could have two oars to row with when required. Before night, I pointed to the heavy swell we were in, remarking that it was a ground swell, and that we could not be very far from land; except my wife and son, they would not have it so; at the same time, I said there was a loom of land ahead, which only caused a murmur. The weather during the night was fine, and the wind light; we kept one oar going, and by keeping the body employed, it relieved the mind from thinking so much on our misery.

My poor wife passed her time during daylight either nursing and tending the little boy, or reading when the weather would admit, our only volume, the best we could have, was the Bible. When our water was done, all we had in the boat drinkable was one pint bottle of Port wine, such as a connoisseur at home would call execrable stuff, why it was so, or in pint bottles, I cannot tell; it was ordered to be the best; besides, I had never before seen pint bottles of wine as ship stores, nor even thought that pints were bottled in bond. But some ship store dealers are not very particular, and it is an easy matter for them to get rid of spurious goods, seamen being very convenient customers for the purpose; for, after having started on their voyage they have to make the best of it. But, if the curses of seamen are of any avail, such dealers have enough called down on their heads to mar their prosperity in this world, and send them into perdition in the next. These remarks do not apply, I hope, to many. There are some that I have dealt with, that I believe are honourable men. Excuse this digression, but of all the stores in the world, water was what we most needed at that time, but of that requisite to animal life we had none.

During the night, we had fine weather, but it was a night to us never to be forgotten, the miserable condition we were in, our dear little boy crying for water the whole night, though we sometimes put a few drops of wine in his mouth; but it had no effect to quench his thirst. We watched as usual for the morning light with great anxiety; but when it did come, and the sun rose, the cry was, "Land, ho!" There truly was the land in sight. We knelt down, and thanked Almighty God for permitting us to behold it once more.

March 26th. The morning opened to us with joy, but the day closed upon us in great sorrow. We had to stir to action, for the land was a long way off, and the wind very light. We got the two oars to work; the morning vapours rising obscured the land again. Some said it was a mistake, I said I was confident, and that we would soon see it again; it fell quite calm.

About 8 a.m. it was breakfast again for those who could eat it, the same fare as we had for some days past. It was part of a Wiltshire cheese, well soaked with salt water, and a little biscuit turned almost into dough by the same. As soon as the repast was ended, we rigged my wife's shawl for an awning to cover the rowers, for the weather was extremely hot, drenching ourselves every few minutes, and drenching the rowers as they sat at the oars.

I told Hall I forgave him his mean, unfeeling conduct, and said, if there was any manliness in him, the poor child's constant cries must go to his heart, and be a great punishment; so work with all your might to get him relief, else he must soon die. For the first time he admitted his guilt, and said he would work as long as he could move. At noon, all were quite satisfied that the land was in sight; but it was yet a long way off. Some of them complained of being hungry; we stopped a few minutes, and let them eat all they could of such as it was, and after it the wine was served, a little to each, still reserving a small quantity for our little boy to moisten his mouth. He was by this time in an awful state; his dear little face was very much scorched and blistered, and altogether [he] was very low and weak; he could not have lived very much longer. His constant cry for water was extremely distressing. My wife, too, was very weak, but seeing the land had cheered her up.

Soon after noon, we got a light breeze of wind, but still we pulled all we could, striving to get to land before dark, for I warned that there would be a heavy surf on the coast, although I had never been there; for this coast of the island being exposed to the south-east trade wind, must certainly have a surf; we pulled hard with what strength there was in us. At sunset, it was the mate's turn steering, I was at the oars. He called to me, saying, it was time I came to steer her in. I went, but I told them I was sorry to have to say we were yet much over a mile from the surf. I scanned the coast, along it there was one unbroken line of surf, I took a bearing of the place where the surf broke nearest the shore, and steered for that spot. We got in close to the surf, when it was getting dark, I told them it would be better for us to keep out for the night, and have daylight to run it, when they all cried out that they could not live until the morning. My poor wife also saying that neither the child or her could live to see the morning light. When I found remonstrance had no effect, I said, "Stop the oars, and let us make our arrangements". I reminded the mate that he had always promised, if he were saved himself, he would save the child, James. I knew he was a splendid swimmer. The two children were passed forward to where he was at the oar, the eldest sitting and holding the little fellow on his knees.

I appealed to them to act like men at the last – to try and save my children, and help each other, saying, at the same time, I would look after my wife. I put a swimming belt on her, the only one we had, and that she had brought herself; and I placed her on the thwart next to myself. These arrangements made, I told them to give way on the oars, our dear little boy cried bitterly. The elder said, "Hush, Jimmy, darling; plenty of water in a few minutes", and commenced singing the evening hymn.

As soon as we got on the back of the surf, my wife said, "Turn back". I replied, "Too late, Mary, give way men, life or death". The first breaker we came to, I saw, would be fatal to our boat, and called out, "We are gone". I could have leaped and cleared the boat, but there were others that I cared for more then myself, the boat turned upon us, and we were a short time under her. I confess I was unable to assist my wife in that position, I was first from under and got out at the stern, I was swimming after her, and from that position could see all. The boy Clarke came from under next, and immediately my wife, on the opposite side. I called to them to get hold of her keel; while I spoke, the boy Radcliffe came out beside Clarke, I could see my wife could not hold long; she had lost hold with one hand. I called to the boys that each should get hold of her hands across the boat. They answered me and did so. Stout was holding on at [the] fore part. Immediately afterwards I had hold, and was just at my wife's side, reaching to take hold of her, when the boat turned over again. We were then all four thrown together, my wife and the boys keeping fast hold of each other, I told them to hold fast, and was behind them swimming, and pushing them in before me. Not more then one minute from this, the boat either turned again, or fell off the sea upon me, giving me a fearful blow, which dislocated some of my ribs. Very shortly after my feet touched ground, between the seas. I then shifted my position, got before them, dragging them in as the sea came, and holding against the drawback. Soon after Stout was rushing in past, I caught hold of him by the waistband of his trousers. He shouted, and screamed to let him go, or he would be drowned. I said, "No! you pull away, my wife and the two boys are drowning", but still he screamed. A very heavy sea passed over us; it loosened my hold on them, and while mending my grip on them I lost his waistband, grasped again, and caught his shirt, he all the time screaming, made a wrench, and left part of his shirt in my hand, and was rushing in through the surf. I thought when he got to the beach, he would turn back to assist us. We were all the time getting nearer in, with hard struggling, for the drawback was very strong. I knew my wife was in the group I was dragging, but I did not know whether she and Radcliffe were living or dead, both having lost their footing; while looking after the retreating form of Stout, pass up the beach and out of sight, I saw a large man walking along the beach line past us. There was still a little light in the western sky, that enabled me to see that he was perfectly naked. I thought it was a native, and called out, "Who is that walking along the beach there?" I got the answer, "It is me, sir". I was astonished, for I recognised the voice to be the mate's. "What you", I said, "walking past and looking at my wife and these boys perishing, if not dead already, come down and help me". At that call he came down, but by the time he got to us, we were near the beach. He helped to carry my wife clear of the water, the boys crawled up with us. As soon as we laid her down, not knowing whether living or dead, I thought the first time about my children. Asked him where they were, thinking he had got them ashore. "They are lost, I suppose", he said. "What", I said, "is that all you know about them?" and rushed out into the surf again near to the boat, which was tumbling about, but could see nothing clinging to her. I returned with a sad heart, and accused him of having deserted my poor children. "At the last, oh! miserable cowards all". He said, "be thankful, sir, you have got your wife". I said, "I know I have got her, either dead or alive, but I have no need to thank you for that; you were passing by looking at me struggling with the three, and would not come down to help until you saw they were through the surf; and not then, until I called you to help in bringing them up". While speaking, I was examining if my wife was alive, and found her still breathing. He said, my children were not the only ones, Thomas Hall was also lost.

We carried my wife further up the beach, where the shore-bank projected and offered a little shelter, and laid her down on the sand. I opened her dress, and tended as well as I could, and she soon showed signs of life. Stout had made his way to this place, and was lying not far off. I accused him of his miserable, cowardly conduct, in making off from us in the surf, leaving a piece of his shirt in my hand, whilst I was struggling to save the three, and not even turning round to see if we had got through. He said, "At such a time as that, it was every man for himself". "You mean, contemptible heap of humanity!" I replied, "You are not worthy to be called a man". We scraped some holes in the sand, as deep as we could, to find water. We then knelt down and prayed, thanking God that he had permitted us to land, and acknowledging His chastening hand in those He had taken away from us. We afterwards examined the holes we had made in the sand, but found no appearance of water. The mate went down the beach to try what he could find that might be washed up from the boat; he found the ensign and blanket which we had used for sails. I took the blanket to cover my wife, the ensign he took to wrap round himself, for he was perfectly nude of everything except shoes. He went again, and found our Bible and the pint bottle that yet had a little wine in it; when he returned, my wife was rallying to consciousness. I must do him the justice to state, that he gave me the bottle with a spoonful of wine in it for her, which I put into her mouth. If the night before was a miserable one, I cannot explain how wretched this night was. We wished for the morning light, yet did not know what to expect when it came. I knew that the southern part of Madagascar was yet in its savage state. The mate had been down to the water's edge again, he complained of being very hungry, and expressing his disappointment at not finding the piece of cheese that was in the boat, he expecting it would be washed up. All he found this last time was an empty pint bottle that had been corked. There was nothing to be seen of our dear children. The last we knew of them was our poor boy singing the lines: "Teach me to live that I may dread the grave as little as my bed", his last words, and the child crying for water when the boat turned over.

My wife sat up while the mate was speaking, and craved for water, saying, if she did not get it soon, she must die. She had heard us talking of our poor children, and although unable to converse, knew of our melancholy loss. The thought just then came into my mind of the traveller's tree, having before read that there was always water to be found in it. I said, "Come, we will try and find it". The mate and the boy Clarke went with me. We found the trees, and there was some water in them; but the great difficulty was to get it, for the night at that time was very dark. We managed very badly at first, losing exceedingly more than we got. The first pint bottle I filled by catching in my mouth, and putting it into the bottle, I must admit letting some down my throat, for it was more than I could resist. Yet we were not very long getting our bottle full, and we hurried back. My wife did not enquire where it came from, but would soon have drained it, had I not asked her to spare some for the boy. Radcliffe was lying prostrate, close by, and craved for some. Stout, hearing that there was water near, called out for some. I said, "No, you must get water for yourself". We went again and succeeded in filling two bottles in a more becoming manner. The tree is something of the nature of the prickly-pear tree. The leaves, if I may so call them, were concave inside, and tapering to a point, being two to three feet long, and containing the water near the stem. The appearance is something like a stunted palm – being a very poor botanist or horticulturist, pardon the description. Most I know is of its prickly character, which hundreds of punctures in our hands, and not a few in our faces, proved. Our new method of filling the bottles was by pulling down one leaf and introducing it into the bottle as a funnel, then breaking the other leaves round at the butt, so that the water ran into it. We got both bottles full, and returned as quickly as possible to my wife and the boy Radcliffe, who soon drained both bottles and wanted more. Stout was calling out to give him some. I said, "No, you shall not have any". He then said, "If I do not get some water, I shall die". "Well, die then', was my answer; "You are far more able than I am to get it for yourself; besides your own principle is, 'every man for himself', but jump up and look for it". He said, "I do not know where to get it". "Well, come along then, and we will show you", was the reply. He was on his feet quick. While away for water this time, the mate asked me, "What land do you think, sir, is this that we are on?", I replied, "You ought to be ashamed to ask that question. You, a man of education, and a navigator, should know that it can be no other land but Madagascar. No wonder I had so much trouble with you all in the boat, not one believing that I knew where we were steering to".

We had a great deal of trouble with Stout in teaching him how to get water from the traveller's tree, he saying he could not get a good drink. I pointed to a tree that we had not touched, and told him to go and help himself. I got my bottles full, and said, "We will return", but told Stout he might stop as long as he pleased; we gave them the two bottles of water. I told my wife that she should have no more, fearing it might have an injurious effect to give her any more at that time. We then rested a little. Some went to sleep, but weary as I was, I could not close my eyes, for my side was very painful; my poor wife was in a very prostrate condition, lying on the sand just as she was dragged out of the surf; we waited anxiously looking to the eastern sky for the daybreak. The atmosphere brightened, and I thought the day was breaking; the tide had receded, leaving the boat dry on the beach. I called them up to go with me, and try to find the remains of our lost ones. We went along about half-a-mile in one direction, but found nothing, we turned back and went in the other direction, about the same distance. Our clothing consisted: the writer, shirt and trousers; boy Clarke the same; Stout, trousers and half a shirt, having very unpolitely left the other with me in the surf. The mate had the only pair of shoes, but no other attire. He still used the ensign as his one robe. As we were returning from our unsuccessful search, we saw a beaten track over the shore bank; we went along it, and were not long until we came to some signs of human habitation, and were soon among several native houses or huts, and a number of cattle in pens; we went to what appeared to us to be the largest of these human abodes, we knocked long and loudly. We could hear some muttering inside, but no one came to answer us. We turned away from this, and went to another of much less pretentions. We found an opening, and something that served as a door. We unceremoniously shoved it open, when at that moment two natives approached us from outside. I caught one of them by the arm and tried to explain by dumb motions that we wanted water. He trembled very much, and did not understand what we wanted. By this time there was a great chattering inside the hut. They soon stirred up the fire, and put some wood on that blazed up; there were men, women, and children. They must have been lying as thick as they could pack, and were now sitting, looking at us in amazement. I stepped over some of them, and advanced up to where the fire was, and found a kind of gourd having some water in it. I seized it and took a drink, then handed it to the rest at the door. The natives looked awfully frightened. The mate's large form in the doorway, wrapt in his red and coloured robe, he looked like a great Warrior Chief. I stepped out after the gourd. As soon as they had emptied it, I put it into one of the natives' hands, and taking hold of him made him understand we wanted it filled again, at the same time telling the rest we must bring some to my wife and the boy Radcliffe on the beach.

By this time the day was breaking. The mate went with me and the native to the well. We got the water. The mate said he would go and get some rice with the others. The native and myself returned to them on the beach. When we drew near to them, I saw a tall native, almost naked, and with a long spear in his hand, standing over them. He made off when he saw me approaching. My wife told me afterwards that the native with the spear gave the boy and her a great fright; and no wonder that he did, for he looked very wild. By this time it was broad daylight. The native with the spear went toward the boat, I followed him, thinking his motive might be plunder. He again made off, as he saw me approach; I found a revolver that was jammed in the stern of the boat, and nothing more. Before daylight the mate had improved his apparel. Finding that the boy Clarke had both drawers and pants he made him part with one of those necessary articles.

I was searching the beach not far from my wife when the rest returned. After eating their rice, there were several natives with them, who took my wife and Radcliffe on their shoulders, and we all went to their village. We were allowed to stop in the dirty, miserable hut that we had at first entered, and there I completely broke down with fatigue and pain; neither my wife or I was able to rise. How my wife was living until this time seemed almost a miracle. This was twelve days she had never changed her clothes and what she had on was wet during the whole time. Many of those days she scarcely tasted food. One of the native women, by motions, induced her to take off her outer garments, that she might get them dried; she took them away for that purpose, but forgot ever to bring them back. While we lay there, a tall, savage-looking native, who the crew had got to know was the chief or proprietor of the village, often came in and squatted himself down, and gave us menacing looks, and took no interest what- ever in relieving us, by having food prepared. The only food that could be had was a little boiled rice, which seemed to be prepared without his orders. We were in a sad condition and did not think that help was so near.

March 27th. About noon, some natives came that had a more civilized look, and fol- lowing them a young man that seemed to have authority. He seemed to be partly European. They called my attention to them. I tried to rise to speak to him; he motioned me to be still, and said "Papa is coming". He could speak only a very few words of English. I said, 'These must be the servants of a missionary'. Our minds were soon set at rest by our very kind friend, Mr Liger, the father of the young gentleman, making his appearance. He had brought some clothes that we might cover ourselves, and saluted us very kindly. He was very angry with the savage-looking chief, ordering him to get us some milk and food. Scolded him very much for keeping us in such a dirty place, compelling the chief himself to wait upon us, not allowing his servants or slaves to perform that service. He seemed almost on the point of flogging the noble chief. I tried again to get up to speak to our kind friend, but was unable. There was plenty of his servants to assist us. Mr L. came to us by land; his son and a number of ser- vants came by a river in canoes. They carried our boat about half a mile overland from the beach, and put her in the river. Before we left the village, I got Mr L. to place two of his servants to watch the beach, if the remains of our lost ones should be cast up, or any of our effects. Our arrangements were soon made, for our baggage was nil. There was a chair had come with Mr Liger for my wife, that she might travel with him over- land. They had brought a bright orange coloured native cloth for a shawl for her, and a most convenient hat, being over three feet diameter, which served the double purpose of an umbrella. Mr Liger and my wife had started before I knew about it, indeed I knew very little of what was going on, for I was very ill at that time. I know that they put me again into our unfortunate boat, the rest of the crew being with me, and Mr Liger's son, with plenty of servants to paddle and bale her out. They were taking us to their own place, the name of which was Mahila. We knew now that the name of the place where we made the fatal landing was Mahila bay, three miles from Mahila, by the coast, but a great deal more by the circuitous river.

About 3 p.m., we arrived at the landing place, Mr Liger was there to meet us, and gave us a hearty welcome, he and my wife having got there long before. Mr Liger, unfortunately for us, could speak only a very few words of English. There was a friend of his with him when we landed, could speak a little; his name, I think, was Mr Augustus. They told us that next morning, a friend of theirs would come to see us, that could speak plenty of English. There was a small house prepared for my wife and me, with female servants to attend her. They had put her into a warm bath before we arrived, which had a very beneficial effect. The beach where we landed was iron sand, which adhered very tenaciously to the skin, and was very painful; it was some time before she got rid of it all from her hair and ears.

There was another house prepared for the crew, where they were attended by men servants, and a cook to prepare their food. As soon as my wife and I were able, we lived with Mr L., sleeping at the house prepared for us. We soon learned that Mr Liger was a native of Mauritius, and was married to a Princess of Madagascar, his wife at the time being on a visit to her sister, the Princess Juliett, at Tamatave. Mr Liger was very much esteemed by all who knew him. He is a man of great wealth, and liberal; and although a Roman Catholic by profession, his house was open to all Protestant missionaries. He is a Judge from whom there is no appeal. We were glad to get to rest, but to sleep was not an easy matter, for our enemy the surf kept up a constant roar, reminding us of our sad loss.

March 28th. This morning, the friend that could speak English, Mr Raphel, also a native of Mauritius, and an English scholar, came to see us. To him we were able to relate all our melancholy disaster. He was exceedingly kind to us. We were then in the midst of kind friends. During the day, several of the respectable natives paid us a visit, and in the evening Mr and Mrs Raphel came to see us. She knew not a word of English, but was very kind to my wife, assisting her in getting some clothes made of such material as the place afforded, and many other kind services. They lived a short distance from Mahila, having to cross an inland salt water lake. They visited us every day, sometimes twice. My wife was very weak, and I had great pain from my shattered ribs. The crew were all weak, but they were well cared for. The mate was the least broken down of us all. We were glad when the visits of the day were over, and went early to rest. Our sleep was much disturbed during the night, for there was a gale of wind, lightning, thunder, and a deluge of rain; and the surf made an awful noise. We felt thankful to the Almighty that we were not at sea in our little boat. Perhaps the reader would like to know the dimensions of our little craft. She was twenty feet long, five feet broad amidship, and twenty inches deep. In her we sailed nearly seven hundred miles. The other boat was twenty-four feet long, but I do not remember her other dimensions.

The rain continued a deluge the whole night, and our house, although a very good one of its sort, was neither wind or water tight, but we were glad to be in it.

March 29th. By the morning light the storm had cleared off, and the sun rose bright and clear. We had a small cup of very good coffee sent to us every morning at daybreak. There were two female servants constantly in attendance on my wife; they slept in the room adjoining our sleeping apartment. Fortunately, looking glasses were not used at Mahila, and very glad I was that my wife was not able to quiz herself, for her face was yet far from being in its natural state, and the native costume was far from elegant.

Some of our friends called early, and before noon, while we were at our house, Mr Liger came to ask us to come to his residence, which was nearly opposite and close to. He said the governor of Mahila was coming on a visit to us. As we crossed we heard music, which neared us, and in a short time was at the door – a motley group of anything but able-bodied troops. These might have been a terror to the natives, but looked contemptible to European eyes. The most of them were armed with old flint-lock Tower muskets of very ancient date. They were dressed up in seedy regimentals, and appeared to be of all ages and sizes; but to take them through, they looked quite as formidable as some Chinese Imperial troops I have seen. On one occasion there was about three hundred of these Imperial troops on the Bund at Shanghai, when I also saw a burly British seaman come out of a ship's chandler's, with sea stores under his arm. Addressing some Europeans that were stood near, he said, "Now, gentlemen, for the small sum of five dollars I will thrash every one of them with a bar of soap", at the same time flourishing his weapon, and making the brave troops fall back.

However, be the Malagasi troops what they may, there was a very active commanding officer. He appeared to do all the duties, from a general down to a non-commissioned officer; but what astonished us most was that he gave the word of command in English. He put this formidable body through evolutions. The fellows doing the music seemed to be blowing with all their might during the review, which lasted about half an hour. As soon as the performance ceased, the governor and his secretary were ushered in. His excellency and secretary wore long top, seedy-looking European hats. They shook hands with us in a friendly manner, their staff following in.

Our friend's reception room was a very large one, but the troops nearly filled it, the commander being among the number. The troops, during his absence, had placed their warlike instruments wherever convenient, and sat at ease outside. We looked at this active officer, having heard him speak our language, expecting him to address us; but we afterwards found out, that had he been pressed to speak English to us, the first word he might have said would be, "to the right about face", for he knew not a sentence, except the word of command to his troops. It is strange, yet we were informed by good authority, that the government correspondence of Madagascar is carried out in English, the only writing they know; and although they can write and understand, few of them can speak a word. We had a clear proof of this, for our passport was written by this same staff in English, and not one of them could speak a word.

Their visit lasted about an hour. Before leaving, they made us presents of rice, fowls and fruit. Having risen to depart, his excellency and superior officers of the staff shook hands with us. It would have been rather a fatiguing business to shake hands with them all, for we were very weak, and the day extremely hot. The commander's appearance was the signal for his brave troops to leap to arms and fall in. The band got up steam, and off they went. All our friends visited us during the day, and were very kind; but our great enemy, the surf, was constantly roaring in our ears, night and day, never for a moment ceasing to remind us of the sad disaster, and the loss of our dear little ones. We had a good look at the bay, and saw that we had run the beach in the very best part, and most clear of reefs. In some places the sea broke more than a mile from the shore, showing that the reefs extended out that far.

Up to this time nothing more was washed up that was in the boat when she was upset. Mr Liger had two servants constantly watching, and such was their report. The Sabbath Day is not at all respected by the Malagasis.

I omitted to remark that I wrote a report on the 28th, Mr Liger having promised to forward it the British Consulate, at Tamatave, which he did. What became of that report I know not, except that it arrived safely at the Consulate; but I have not seen anything resembling it in print.

March 30th. Our friends paid us a visit early. I spoke to Mr Liger about getting on our way to Tamatave, being the nearest seaport. His advice was, that we should remain at Mahila until the British Consul sent for us. We thought it would be too long to wait, and if it were possible, we preferred getting on our way. He said, if we so wished, he would send us; he at the same time remarking, that it would be a very tedious and fatiguing journey, and occupy more than twelve days. Yet we were anxious to be on our way towards home. We asked how soon it would be convenient for him to send us. He answered, in three days. I saw by his chart, the distance was three degrees latitude to Tamatave, being one hundred and eighty miles; but was informed that circuitous routes would make the distance two hundred and sixty miles.

During the day, news came to Mr Liger that our little boat had landed on the beach, about thirty miles from us, but there was only eight men landed. Preparations were soon made for Mr Liger's son to go to look for them. We consulted what was best to be done. It would take two days to get to them. They were thirty miles nearer Tamatave than we were. It was decided that they should proceed to Tamatave, Mr Liger said he would send servants to look after and provide for them. I wrote to them to be entirely guided by the bearers, who would forward them to the nearest British Consulate, and seaport, and would send servants with them to provide for their wants on the journey; that we were thirty miles further off than they, and would start on our way three days from date of advice, and to let me know who of their number was lost, there being one short, by the news we had received of them. Mr Liger's son started on his errand of mercy about noon. What makes travelling so slow, is, that the natives refuse to go on the rivers by night; and no wonder, for the rivers swarm with crocodiles. These monsters attack small canoes, and smash them up to get at the freight. We were informed that many hundreds, if not thousands, of the poor natives become their food every year. During the afternoon there were messengers arrived at Mahila with an invitation for my wife and me to visit and spend a few days with the district governor. There was also a large escort to take us safely through our journey.

Our very kind friend, Mr Liger, informed us that it was a very fine place, and a beautiful country; but also told us it would take two days to travel there. On learning that, we declined the kind invitation, with thanks. Had we been in less melancholy circumstances we might have accepted his excellency's proffered kindness; but as it was with us at the time, we preferred getting on our way homeward.

I before said that Mr L. knew very little of our language, so our conversation was carried on through the interpretation of our mutual friend, Mr Raphel.

I also stated Mr Liger was a Judge; I had the honour on several occasions of sitting beside him on his judicial bench, in the verandah. The court was orderly conducted, no legal practitioners, if there be such in Madagascar, were ever allowed admission. If there be any of the professon, I fear they do not carry on a profitable business, for there were neither briefs, deeds, or documents of any description used, nor yet a record kept. The clients appeared to be allowed only one witness each inside, their friends remained outside the court, and dare not interfere with the business going on; but if either wished to consult their friends, they could go out and do so. Judgment always appeared to give satisfaction. The defaulters had to pay the costs, which did not require being taxed; if both were to blame, both had to pay. Their manner of doing so was by handing the Judge some silver; he took a little, and passed it back again. The charges were very light.

The current coin of the country appeared to be French dollars, and the natives have a convenient way of turning them into small change, by cutting them into pieces; so that money weight and scales are a requisite to every person in dealing.

March 31st. The time began to hang very heavily on our hands, and although nothing could exceed the kindness of our friends, who argued that we were too weak and ill to travel, yet we were anxious to be on our way homeward. The second of April was the day arranged for our departure, but on this day Mr Liger informed us that we could not get away until the fourth, his own largest canoes being away with Mrs Liger he had to send a considerable distance to get one that would suit, to fit a cover over part of it, for my wife's greater comfort and convenience. Our friends were slave owners; Mr Liger owned a great number. Slavery is carried on to a great extent, but in the mildest form I have seen; and slaves are cheap, about thirty dollars each, male and female the same; I do not think there are slave auction marts in Madagascar. I have witnessed slave sales by auction, and it seemed very cruel to see intending purchasers handling them as dealers would a horse or a cow in our own country, with only one exception; here intending purchasers would take the animal by the jaw to examine the mouth; the slave was told to show his ivory.

April 1st. We had very heavy rain at intervals; the natives were getting used to our pale faces, and did not stare so much.

April 2nd. The canoe arrived, and was being fitted up for our accommodation.

April 3rd. Before noon, the governor of Mahila and his staff, troops, and band, came to bid us farewell, all the same as before, with additional numbers. They went through the same review. Refreshments were served to those of superior grade. After remaining about one hour, they made us presents as before, and took their departure.

We were pleased that we had not started on the second, as had been first arranged, for I was called aside by Mr Liger during the afternoon, to see a portion of my elder son's remains, the refuse of sharks or voracious fish. His head was gone; all that was left was the trunk of his body and the leg and arm bones. I requested that we might see his remains interred before we started on our journey. Mr Liger promised that it should be as we wished, and gave the necessary order to have a coffin made, and a grave ready. My poor wife was anxious to see his remains, but I would not allow her. We carved a rude inscription on a piece of board to erect over his place of burial.

Before night, Mr Liger's son returned, having brought back with him the second mate; I enquired of him why he came to us, having increased his journey so much, for that we should start next day on our way to Tamatave, going back over the same ground. He replied, he was glad to be able to get away from the men, they were conducting themselves so badly. He further stated that it was the carpenter that was lost from their boat. He took to drinking sea water, and jumped overboard in a state of delirium, the same morning they made the land; I enquired if they made efforts to save him. He said, they did go back to him; he was floating on the surface of the water, but was quite dead. He further informed me that they effected a good landing on the evening of the 27th, the day after us, with daylight, and before the storm commenced. They saved their lives, but lost all they had in the boat, in the devouring surf. They had escaped the bad weather that we had experienced, from which I presume they had not got so near the island of Bourbon as we were, and the storms we had were close to that island.

He said they spent an awful time in their boat; that the men were quarrelling and fighting most of their time. A few days before they made the land, the cook proposed prayer. One that was a Romanist objected, saying, "Every man must pray for himself". However, the cook prevailed. A remarkable instance of Providence occurred to them two days before they saw land; they found a full bottle of wine corked tight and floating on the sea.

Mr Liger told us that all would be ready for our departure on the morrow, that he would send one of his own cooks to prepare our food, and a female servant to attend my wife. We would have the necessaries with us, and whatever more was required, one of his principal servants that was going with us would have means to purchase. He also offered me money, which I refused, thinking we had taxed his kindness too much already. I had previously written to the Consulate of Tamatave, that we would start on our journey on the 2nd, to stop them sending for us, and to give them an opportunity of sending messengers to meet us.

April 4th. We rose early, after a sleepless night, knowing the sad duty we had to perform. All was ready. A grave was dug in their little Christian burial ground or cemetery; and although all our friends were Romanists, there was no sectarian prejudices, for his grave was dug near to the remains of a departed priest of their profession. My poor boy's remains were enclosed in a good hardwood coffin. We had neither minister or book of common prayer, consequently, no burial service for the dead. Our Bible was the only book we had. Our friends paid the greatest respect to his remains. After this last sad service, we placed the inscription to our dear boy's memory. Mr Liger promised that he would have the beach watched for ten days longer, and if any portion of his little brother's remains were cast up, [they] should be placed in the same grave with him, or, if the seaman, [he] should also have a place in their cemetery, and that he would have our dear boy's grave railed in immediately.

We were soon ready, with sad hearts, to take our departure. Our friends all accompanied us to the landing place, where there was already a number of natives waiting to bid us farewell. Three canoes were in waiting ready for us to embark. The canoes were manned by twenty of Mr Liger's servants to paddle us along. Our servant that acted as steward, our female servant, and Hova or government officer, and one in charge of the whole, was of European extraction; but not one of them could speak a word of English, and two native female passengers. All the cooking utensils, ware, and cutlery, bed and bedding for my wife.

Thc crew were supposed to use the native service, which were large leaves, the name of which I do not remember, but which answered as dishes, plates, cups, spoons, or anything else in the line of native service, and were always clean, the same service never being used twice. All being now ready, we bade our kind friends farewell, the ladies shedding tears on the occasion – Mr Liger superintending the embarkation. The canoe with the cover was for the use of my wife and myself, but finding we could make room for one of the boys under the cover, we took one with us, having them in turns about at every station where we stopped. The natives seemed in high spirits at starting, as if going for a month's excursion, but we were very sad, and my state of mind was not improved when it was intimated by our kind friends that my wife might break down with fever on the way.

We started at a good speed over the inland sea, the natives trying their strength in a race to begin with. The day was exceedingly hot, but there was a light breeze, which made it more bearable, so long as it continued with us. After we had crossed the lake, or inland sea, we went along a fine river for one or two hours, and then entered a narrow and critical passage, where no breath of wind could reach us. The passage was so obstructed by fallen trees, on which our canoes sometimes grounded, and very often stuck in the mud on the banks. The foul odour of decayed vegetables and trees, and the extreme heat, rendered the atmosphere almost unbearable. I thought, if much of our journey were to be like this, more than my wife might soon break down. We tried in vain to get to know how long this state of slow suffocation would last; but after some two or three hours, we got through into another fine and open river, which was a great relief. In half-an-hour afterwards, we arrived at a village on its banks, where we were to

remain for the night. Our canoes were discharged of the chattels, the baggage was easily removed; all they contained were carried up to the village, where cooking operations were soon commenced to provide us a supper. The villagers, as might be expected, all turned out to have a look at us. A house or hut was soon made ready for us, and
another for the crew. All the furniture these abodes could boast was matting on the
floor, of doubtful cleanliness, and two or three large stones to serve as a fireplace. We
had much preferred the ground for the floor, if it had been clean.

We now took the mate into our mess and lodging. The two boys we also took to
lodge with us, but we could not accommodate them at mess. Mr Liger had thoughtfully sent a curtain along with the mattress, which was a great boon to us, for inside the
curtain my wife had to perform her toilet, and it served to protect us while we slept
from the hungry mosquitoes, centipedes, and tarantulas. Our friends at Mahila had also
supplied us with a change of clothes, of such as were used in that country, each of us
having two suits. We had for supper boiled rice, fowls, and sometimes fish or fruit. There
was very little bread to be had at Mahila, all they could collect for us being about two
pounds of small biscuits, part of which was got from the governor. They expected to
get their fresh supply daily, as the season had commenced for vessels trading on the
coast. After supper, we soon went to rest – the surf was roaring not far off. I was up
early and disturbed the rest, thinking it was daybreak. We went to get up the servants,
which was not very soon accomplished.

April 5th. We were ready to start some time before daylight. The canoes were hauled
up and turned over to get the water out, for it had rained very heavy during the night.
They were put afloat again. We all got packed in, and started, the natives keeping up a
constant yelling noise, I suppose to keep away the crocodiles. We were on this fine river
until about noon, when we came to a village – here we landed to take breakfast, which
was a repetition of supper the evening before.

After breakfast, as soon as our sable crew could be mustered, which always took a
long time, we again started. Sometimes we traversed, at other times crossed, beautiful
rivers, and sometimes we had very critical navigation. There were some of the rivers
broad and grand, but very little current in any of them, I suppose through the surf banking up their mouth where they discharged into the sea. We often passed openings,
where our enemy was surging and roaring, and in some places breaking from twelve to
fifteen feet high, although at the time it appeared calm outside. We were in no mood
for enjoying the beautiful scenery passed through, for my poor wife was very weak and
ill, and my shattered ribs were still very painful, and our mode of conveyance was very
monotonous, for we had either to sit still or lie down; if we moved to change our posi-

tion, or even to move a leg, there was a murmur of disapprobation from the natives, fearing our canoe would turn over and leave us all struggling in the water at the mercy of the crocodiles and sharks – for, strange as it may appear, some of these rivers abounded with both. Indeed, I think at times we would have enjoyed the change of having a shaking up, even in a mule cart, if our hands were not fast, but there is neither horse, mule or donkey to be seen in Madagascar.

Before sunset, we arrived at the village where we were to spend the night. All the inhabitants soon appeared to be on the river banks, to gaze upon us as human, I fear miserable-looking specimens of our northern clime; and, no doubt, had we landed in one of our ports at home in our then costume, we should have been gazed at as human curiosities, especially my wife, her anything but fashionable dress, and hat three feet or more in diameter.

With the exception of staring, the natives were harmless and inoffensive. We did not adopt the system that the crew of the other boat practised at first, when their health permitted. We were informed that when they landed near a village, they took it by storm, by giving a shout and run. The inhabitants, seeing them coming, deserted their village, and left them the undisputed right to help themselves to all they could find. We went among them peaceably, and were kindly treated at nearly all the villages. The chiefs and Hovas made us presents of rice or fowls, fruit, sugar-cane, and sometimes a few eggs. It was dark before our dinner was ready, [after] which, when we had partaken, we went to rest.

April 6th. We were again early astir, and ready to start before daylight, after spending a long time in getting our natives mustered. Some of the huts we stopped at, or government rest-houses, of which there was one in every village, were filthy places. The cost of building a first-class house of this description, we were informed, was five dollars, or twenty shillings sterling. We stopped for breakfast as before, and before dark arrived at the village where we spent the night. At many of the villages we could gather wild oranges, and always plenty of cocoa nuts. Some of the rivers and banks were beautiful with overhanging trees and plants, and some places flowers. We saw many birds of splendid plumage, and often the beautiful king-fisher in his haunt.

April 7th. We rose early, and started before daylight. Our travelling was something similar to the day previous. We saw abundance of game, our European had an old fowling-piece with him, and until his ammunition was consumed, he sometimes got us some teal and ducks. Our mode of travelling was very wearisome, and my wife was very weak, but tried to keep up her spirits. The village at which we stopped for the night appeared to be the largest we had yet stopped at. The natives serenaded us, and kept up singing and dancing near our hut [a] great part of the night, their unmelodious harmony keeping us awake.

April 8th. We rose early as usual, but had great difficulty in getting our native force up, I suppose, through their having joined in the festivities of the night; for they appeared to have plenty of native intoxicating drinks amongst them; but we got away by daybreak. This was a memorable day to the Malagasis, for the news had reached the village where we were to spend the night, that their queen (whether beloved or not, I cannot tell) was dead, and perforce all her Majesty's subjects must go into deep and dirty mourning. The two female passengers gave vent to their sorrow in long and loud yells, not so much I believe for the loss of their sable queen, as the mourning they must perform. They pulled down their short curly black tresses, to take a last fond look, for they must immediately lose them. The natives high and low, male and female, must all be close cropped or shaved and it would have been a great benefit to the whole community if it were carried out every month of their lives, saving them a great amount of labour and irritation. If any of the European merchants of human hair had visited Madagascar at that time, they might (if the staple of the article had suited the home market) have done a large and profitable business, for heaps of curly black hair were to be seen wherever there was any dwelling; after having their heads shorn of the black crop and stock, they must remain uncovered for one month, not even allowed to hold an umbrella over them. That was the clean part of the mourning. The dirty part was carried to a great extent; they were not allowed to wash any part of their skin, nor change their garments, or eat with anything but their hands, or the native service, the leaves before mentioned. They were not allowed to sit or sleep on anything but mats on the floor. Besides all this, they had to do real mourning certain days every week, by assembling in the garrison towns, or where there was a governor or superior officer, there to mourn for their departed queen on their knees; and we were well informed that the mourner had to shed tears, which if they could not for sorrow, they must for pain. The Hovas going amongst them, armed with bamboos, laid on their backs until they cried out; we ourselves saw large crowds from the village, escorted by the chief and hovas, to the place of mourning. This mourning business was certain to continue a month, and how much longer they did not know. Our native force were soon shorn and much altered in appearance, not being allowed to wear anything but the original native dress, which was not extensive. Straw hats were at a great discount. They amused themselves by kicking them about until they were destroyed. Our European, having something of the native in his composition, had to mourn like the others.

The latter part of this day's journey was very severe upon us. We had to pass through an immense swamp, all of us, except my wife, having to walk and sometimes wade up to our knees in mud, and through long rushes. The natives dragging the canoes through places like dirty ditches. It was a great relief to get away from this great swamp, and to the village, where we remained for the night; so far on our journey, the weather had been favourable. There had been heavy rains every night, but it was fair weather during the day.

April 9th. We rose and started early. Before daylight we came to a stop, where the canoes were to be carried over a hill to another river. Mr Liger had sent two light constructed chairs with us, that my wife and me should at such places be carried; but the natives had by this time made up their minds to do no more than they could help. We had to walk. We were both almost broken down before we got over, having to rest several times. My poor wife was very weak, and my side was very painful. The rest of our party were travelling on a little before us. They met a French gentleman, Mr Lewell, being the first European we had met on our journey. He could speak a little English, and sympathised with us in our distress. He was a trader travelling in the opposite direction, he turned back with us to the place where he had spent the night, which was not far off. He ordered his servants to make us some tea, and offered us such refreshments as he had with him. He was exceedingly kind; said he would turn back with us to Mahanaro, where he resided, and [which] was the place intended that our party should spend the next night. He came with us in our canoe. He informed us that there was an Englishman lived at the same place, a Mr Oakes; he inquired how long we had been on our journey. On being told, he said we had made very slow progress.

When we got to the village where we were to breakfast, he said, our canoes were going very slow, and advised that we should go with him in his canoe, to get along faster. We did so, and left the village without stopping to breakfast, leaving the rest of our party at that place of mourning to get their much needed repast. On our passage, we came to a large and rapid river, we crossed near the mouth, where our old enemy was roaring and surging, keeping it banked in. Our friend informed us that there were immense waterfalls of great grandeur a few miles further up; but in our weak and miserable state, we had no wish to visit them; but after crossing over, soon turned into a smaller stream, which was running rapidly in our favour. After passing through it, we came to another large river, and after a great deal of traverse sailing, arrived at Mahanaro, early in the afternoon.

Mr Oakes lived in the same compound with Mr Lewell, who soon came to see us, after landing, and we were very kindly entertained. The rest of our party arrived a few hours after us. We enquired if they had seen or heard of our other boat's crew, that should have passed through four or five days before; they said they had not heard anything of them.

These gentlemen wished us to stop a few day with them, to recruit our strength; but whether they had proposed this or not, our native forces were determined to have one day's rest, and they also said the Hovas would compel them to stop and do a day's mourning at the place.

Mr Lewell said such travelling would not do for my wife, we had not yet done more than one-third [of] the journey. He was sure if we still went on by the canoes, that my wife would be dead before we got to Tamatave. So it was arranged, that after one day's rest, my wife and I should go in chairs. By this arrangement, others would be enabled to travel much faster, by leaving the large canoe behind: for previously they had to make two journeys in carrying the canoes, for it took all the native force to carry the large one, then they went back for the other two.

This place was very close to the shore bank, where the surf kept up its constant roar. We had only to look out at the door of our hut, and see it foaming, breaking, and dashing in, fit to destroy anything that came in its way.

Mahanaro boasted in a place called by Europeans a castle; its situation was on a high precipitous headland. Except on the land side, we could see its flagstaff by looking almost straight up from the hut we occupied; inside its mud walls was the place of mourning, where the natives had to assemble to do the crying business.

April 10th. I thought it would be difficult for my wife and me to travel alone with the natives, not being able to speak a word to them. We wished Mr Oakes to accompany us to the nearest missionary station. He at first hesitated, and said he had urgent business to attend to. Mr Lewell said, if it were requisite, he would attend to the business for him; and if he did not go, he, Mr. L., would go with us, which at once decided the question that Mr Oakes would go with us, travelling in chairs carried on the backs of natives. It is a mode of conveyance I never did like, and very few times practised, but on the present occasion it was a necessity.

April 11th. An early breakfast was prepared, and the crew were started off, about an hour after sunrise, in two canoes. The day's rest had a beneficial effect upon us all. About 8 a.m. the Hovas of Mahanaro came to us, having been informed the day before that bearers were required to take us to Tamatave. They told our friends that they would soon bring all the bearers required. They went away for that purpose, returning about an hour after with a number of natives. By that time the day was so far advanced that it was arranged that the bearers should have breakfast before they started. Accordingly, breakfast was prepared for them, which, as soon as they had eaten, they were mustered for a start; but the Hovas, whom our friends had regaled with something stronger than tea, spoiled our start, by informing our bearers that they must work for "Pun, Pun!" – which meant no pay, otherwise for government account – for that is the way the government pay for all labour. Although our friends asssured the bearers that Consul Pakenham would pay, yet a number of them made off, and we saw them no more, but had some fourteen bearers, whereas we ought to have had twice that number. Then those that did remain must have their kabara, which was about half-an-hour's dispute amongst themselves. They could see at a glance which would be the greatest burthen, and all of them wanted to carry my wife. Unfortunately, my proportions were a great disadvantage to me in chair travelling, and I had to make a reasonable allowance for nearly always being in the rear, sometimes to a very uncomfortable extent, for they often ran off with my wife far out of sight.

Through the delays before mentioned, we did not get away until about noon.

I ought to inform the reader, who may not be acquainted with the history of Madagascar, that the Hovas, so often mentioned, are the ruling tribe. They appear to be of Malay origin, and although their numbers appear small, keep the Malagasis in great subjection.

The natives, as a whole, appear to be very timid and inoffensive people, more so than any tropical nation I have ever known. The weather was very gloomy when we started, and before we had been one hour on our way, the rain poured down in torrents. We had umbrellas that served to keep the force of it off when we could hold them up, but often we were taken through jungle and branches of trees, and it was for ourselves to look out for both umbrellas and our heads. As we dashed through, it was like an uncomfortable shower-bath; all our thin clothing was soon soaked to their utmost; but on we went, for if we stopped, there must be a long kabara before we got started again, that might take up a great deal of time; or worse, our bearers might bolt and leave us. Sometimes they dashed through streams or pools, up to their waist in water, and we had to look out for our legs. And this was our travelling by the road to Tamatave, save the mark, we never saw anything like a road, and very seldom a beaten track; yet we were travelling on the highway between Tamatave, the principal sea-port, and the capital Antananarivo. During the afternoon, we came up to the the rest of our party, while they were landing, for to carry their canoes about one mile or more. Half-an-hour afterwards, we came to a village where our bearers came to a standstill.

My wife and me were in advance of our friend. The bearers put us down, and left us. The rain had by that time ceased, but the water was dripping from my wife's clothes.

On our way we had augmented our force with three or four more bearers, but they were still dissatisfied. There was at the time a breeze of wind, and my wife, with her wet clothing, was shivering with cold. I went through the small village, and saw some Malabars in a shop, that could speak a little English; they saw my wife very wet and cold, invited us to sit down in their shop. Native grog seemed to be their principal stock; they made some of it hot, but we could not taste it, the smell was enough. They got some milk and made that hot; we soon took that, and thanked them for it. By the time we got the milk, Mr Oakes had got up to us; the bearers set him down also, and had a long kabara, and would move no further. At length, Mr Oakes found out that one of Mr Liger's servants had followed us, and was then in the crowd inciting our bearers to rebel. He wanted, I suppose, to detain us all he could, that the canoes might get before us. I gave him a hint as well as I could to leave our force; he attended to it, and made off. Yet still, the bearers were determined not to move, we had not very far to travel to the village where we would spend the night, which could be reached either by land or water. The Malabars proffered to lend us a canoe, which we accepted. We got our chairs into it. When the bearers saw we were off, some of them soon got in to paddle us along, the remainder set off along the bank. We reached the village as it was getting dark, by which time our clothes had nearly dried upon us. We had a little dinner, and soon went to our hut for the night. The village chief and Hovas brought us presents of rice, fowls, and a young pig, all of which we left with the woman who had accommodated us by cooking our dinner and [providing] a hut to sleep in. Mr Oakes had a promise from the village chief, that he would send plenty of bearers before sunrise next morning. The rest of our party arrived about two hours after us. The female servant had travelled by the canoes, but found out our hut, and came there to sleep, having very thoughtfully brought the mosquito curtain.

April 12th. We rose some time before daylight, had a cup of tea, and were ready for our journey; there were a good number of bearers, but their kabara lasted so long that we thought they were not going to take us. I enquired about the canoes, but was informed that they had left some hours before. The bearers' kabara, I think, must have lasted two hours; my proportions were again unfavourable to me; although not a large man, and in the reduced condition I was in, my weight could not be much over twelve stone. Yet, for the occasion, I would have been glad to have been two or three stone less. At length I picked the lightest chair, and after another short kabara, we got away again much short of our complement of bearers. It commenced to rain immediately after we started, and soon poured down in torrents. We were not long until again all our thin clothing was as wet as possible. The scenery we passed through was beautiful, sometimes through groves of wild orange trees, loaded with fruit; but if we could then have the privilege of choice, we would have preferred clear roads, instead of being drenched among the dripping branches; we sometimes travelled by river banks, at other times through forest groves and jungle, and sometimes on the beach, close to the surf, the roar of which we scarcely ever lost the sound during our waking hours; many were the blows we had on both head and face by the overhanging branches. The torrent of rain continued till about noon, when we came to the bank of a large river, which we had to cross. On the opposite side was the village where we had to take breakfast. We saw the rest of our party paddling to the village, my wife and me were much in advance of our friend. Some canoes were lying at the bank, ready to do a ferry business. We and our force got into two of them, and crossed over. When we got to the village, we were waiting for our friend, for we had no money to pay the ferry. We felt very wet, cold, and wretched, and did not know which way to turn; but seeing a European, we walked towards him; he also advanced to meet us. We found him to be a Frenchman, who could speak very few words of our language, but intimated that his wife could speak it, and conducted us to their house. His wife appeared to be a native of India, [and] could speak English pretty well. Shortly after we got to the village, the rain having ceased, the sun shone out brightly. We asked the woman to lend my wife some clothing to cover her, and she took off every article of clothing, and I hung them up in the sun to dry, not forgetting to do the same with my own. Mr Oakes soon after reached the village, and soon found us out. Both the man and his wife were very kind, and had our breakfast cooked for us. It took the Frenchman a great part of the time running out with his gun to keep back the crowd. This being a large village, all the inhabitants wanted to have a look at the white woman; by the time our breakfast was ready, our clothes were quite dry.

Here our friend told us that he would only travel with us to the end of this day's journey, but that the next place we should remain for the night, was a French gentleman's place, at Marsec, who was a very kind man. He would send us on our way another day's journey, which would bring us to the first or nearest missionary station, Andovoranto. This news damped our spirits. We thought our friend was breaking down; he looked ill. We dreaded having to be left to the natives' mercy alone, not knowing their language.

Breakfast over, we started again, having increased our forces. Through the services of the village chief, we had our full complement, but only for the single journey to Marsec. With our full force of bearers, we made good progress, and arrived at Captain Gano's, in Marsec, before dark; our kind entertainer had been a shipmaster, but was then in business at that place. He received us very kindly, and when asked if he would send us to Andovoranto, he unhesitatingly replied that he would, with great pleasure send plenty of bearers, and a European that could talk a little English. Captain G. could speak our language pretty well, and was indeed all that Mr Oakes had said, exceedingly kind. Soon after our arrival at Marsec, the Hovas paid us a visit, and made us presents of rice, fowls, a goose, and turkey. We told our new friend that these presents must be his; we could not take them along with us. The rice, he said, we could take with us, as a supply for our bearers the next day, and the turkey could be cooked for our own use on the journey. He gave orders that it should be prepared for us; but his native housekeeper, having an eye to business, said it was not requisite, as she had a cold duck that we might take with us. This settled the question, and the turkey was left to live a little longer. The female servant travelling with us on foot the last stage, trotted along as well as the best of them, but had no burden to carry; she got our mosquito curtain up in a clean little room while we were at dinner. We could not speak too highly of the kind attention and faithfulness of this poor creature to my wife; soon after dinner we went to rest.

April 13th. We were up early, and after having a cup of coffee, we were again ready to start. This place was on the bank of a fine river, and not far from the beach, where the surf as usual was roaring.

Mr. Gano sent most of the bearers across the river. He told us that there was a large forest on the opposite side, which rendered it difficult for chair travelling, and arranged that we should proceed up the river a few miles by canoe before landing. Before sunrise we bade our friends farewell and left. Our European guide was in charge of the canoe; he appeared to be of Portuguese origin, and could speak a few words of our language. After proceeding four or five miles up the river, we landed on the bank, where the bearers were waiting for us. There was plenty of them, I think more than thirty; yet they must have their kabara, and a long one it was. The strife was again who should carry my wife; the guide pointed out one man who was making all the mischief among them. He had travelled from Mahanaro with us. To restore order, I gave him a broad hint to go away, which he did. We then got started. We soon learned something from our guide that saved our heads considerably. Observing him, when he came to branches that were likely to come in contact with the upper members of his body, he called out a word that caused the bearers to stoop; we soon picked up the word, and used it to a good effect; we had only travelled about two hours, when we came to another river, that we must cross. There was only two small canoes to ferry us over, which would only take two or three passengers each at one time. We should have had great detention, had not the bearers all jumped into the river in a body; and making a great noise,

I suppose to keep their long-jawed enemies at a distance, while they swam across. When we all got over, there was another kabara before they would go on again. In fact, wherever the chairs were put down, there must be a kabara before starting again.

About noon we arrived at a little miserable and almost deserted village, at which we were to breakfast. When ready, we sat down, expecting to have some cold duck; but when it was turned out, there was only the ribs and truckles of one that had been on the table the evening before at dinner, and it appeared as if the native housekeeper, or her friends, had been enjoying the remains, mourning fashion. We left it for our guide and female to devour, and satisfied ourselves with a little boiled rice; the natives devour all the fowl bones.

At this place we lost about two hours, through the bearers being so long feeding; their pots being too small, they boiled them two or three times over, before they had enough rice.

After the usual kabara, we got on the way again. Most of the afternoon we travelled by the bank of a large lake or inland sea, studded in some parts with beautiful little islands, after passing which, we came to a decrepit wooden bridge, over which it was dangerous to pass. This was the first attempt at bridging we had seen in Madagascar, and it was the worst attempt I had ever seen. Close by was a noble river, and our guide pointed out Andovoranto on the opposite side, where the missionary station was, and where we very much desired to be. But over this river was a government ferry, and none must cross it without the governor's permission. His residence was not far off. There we must go, and show ourselves. We got to the entrance gate, where some dirty, or mourning soldiers were lounging about. His excellency was informed, and we were ordered to put in an appearance. We were carried forward through a large compound to government house, a large shed, with a partial partition or division, but with plenty of open space, to see all the cooking going on from the council chamber. His excellency was seated on a mat on the floor, with a long row of officials on his right, all in deep mourning, holding their place according to rank. He rose as we entered, advanced, and shook hands with us, and saluted us very kindly. The superior officers followed his example. They handed us chairs, of which article of household goods I think there was only three, with two long forms, and a deal table, were all the furniture we could see in the palace, for I was informed that her majesty sometime since dwelt there for change of air. His excellency and staff having settled down into their mourning position, commenced a long kabara, with a great deal of whispering. Our guide informed us that these authorities had been officially advised of our coming that way.

I told our guide to hurry up to his excellency, as we wanted to get across the river before dark. He then started his secretary to write out our passport, the writer making slow progress, his excellency having to teach him, and take a spell at the writing. I got impatient, and rose up to leave, but he begged us to wait a little. Some of his staff went out, and soon returned with presents of rice, fowls, and about a quarter of beef with the skin and hair on. When our bearers got hold of these presents, they looked upon them as their perquisites, and we saw them no more.

These authorities all rose and shook hands with us. We took our departure, and hurried to the ferry, but those in charge of the canoes were not in a hurry. After being delayed some time, we got away. This river was a very fine one. We crossed near the mouth, where the surf was working all the time, keeping it banked in.

It was nearly dark before we got across the finest river we had yet seen. We landed at the village, and for the first time our bearers started without a kabara, but the mission house was close by. Some messengers had run before us to give them the news. We had passed through the entrance gate, and were proceeding through the compound. My wife as usual was in the front. The Rev Thomas Campbell had come out to meet us. When he saw my wife: "What", he exclaimed, "do I see my country woman in such distress, come in". Tears and emotion choked his utterance for some time. Here we had a true English welcome. One of the first questions we asked was, if he would escort us to Tamatave? Without hesitation, he replied, "I will, with very great pleasure". I remarked, "You do well to say so", for we had determined that the first missionary we met must do so, or we would thrust ourselves on his hospitality, until the consul sent for us. He was very indignant with the consular authorities, in not having informed him of the sad occurrence, and our travelling that way, for, had he known, he would certainly have gone to meet us. He very much desired us to stop a few days with him, to rest and recruit our health, but we were anxious to be getting homeward, and wished to be on our way next morning. Immediately after we got to the mission house, some Hovas arrived from Tamatave with a letter from the British vice-consul, who had very kindly sent by them a present of useful stores for our journey, which some days before would have been a great addition to our fare; but we were then well cared for at the mission house, for Mr C. offered us all and everything he had.

The Hovas offered to render any further services they could. They said that was their orders. Mr Campbell asked if we required any more of them; I replied that he knew best, we put ourselves in his hands to see us to Tamatave, and if he did not require their services, to send them to meet the rest of our party, and assist them. He did so. He was very angry with them for being so long on the road, five days, whereas they should have passed through Andovoranto three days before. Mr C. went to look after the European that had been our guide, that he might entertain him and his bearers, but was informed that he had gone to the place of a friend, and taken all his bearers with him. He also wondered that our bearers had not gone to look for food. I told him they would not be short, for they had all the presents we had from the governor and his staff. We had dinner, and afterwards related our melancholy catastrophe to him. He told us that his fellow-worker and partner, Mr Maundrell, had some months before gone to Mauritius to recruit his broken-down health, and by his last letter he expected him soon back. He said he missed him very much, for they had been close partners and companions in privation and dangers for four years. He would not return alone, but was bringing a partner with him, that would be a closer companion than he had been; and he had been very busy trying to get their new house finished and all in order by the time Mrs Maundrell arrived. He would then leave the station to them, and travel to extend their mission. We conversed until a late hour, for we felt ourselves so much at home that we forgot bed time, and after prayers, it was midnight before we retired. I must say that all the Frenchmen we had met, up to this time, were as kind to us as our own countrymen would have been, and it was chiefly their kindness that took us thus far.

April 14th. We rose at an early hour, and soon after had a light breakfast. It was a sumptuous repast to us, after so long getting none until about noon, although we rose very early. Mr Campbell soon commenced to make arrangements for our departure. He sent a servant into the village to get bearers. In a short time some came, but not enough. He sent them back to bring more along with them, for we required twenty, having only seven that came the whole journey with us. At this time the bell of the little church was tolling for early morning prayers, Mr C. excused himself to go and conduct the service. While he was attending to his congregation, we took a look round the mission house. It was the best house we had yet seen, situated in a large compound. The little church was close by, and our old enemy, the surf, was not far off with its constant roar. There was only a little jungle at the rear of the house that prevented a full view of it. Some natives were cutting a large opening in this jungle, to allow the sea breeze to blow fairly on the mission house. When Mr C. returned from the church, there was plenty of bearers had arrived at the compound. Mr Campbell tried to engage them at the proper rate; but they demanded some three times that amount; and I have no doubt they gave him a great deal of insolence, but he only smiled. He seemed to be the right man in the right place, for he has a very large amount of patience but also firmness. After many kabaras, and going away, of which he took no notice, eventually they returned, and accepted the proper terms. He told them the conditions, that they were to bring us to Tamatave by the next evening. Then he gave them some money to get their breakfast.

While Mr C. was making terms with the bearers, a great number of his native converts and congregation had assembled to take leave of their pastor, bringing presents of fruit and flowers for him and us. They seemed very much attached to him, and I think no one could know him without liking him. Also, I observed that the women who brought bananas, forced their children to pull some off and eat them. I asked the reason. He said it was to let us see that the fruit was not poisoned. Mr C. said he would have liked to improve my costume, but the great difference in our proportions would not admit of it, he being about the right size and weight for chair travelling. We had a good substantial breakfast; and the bearers having mustered, Mr C. enquired particularly if they had taken plenty of breakfast. They all answered, yes. He then took a list of their names that were to bear us.

By this time twice as many, if required, were ready to go. He only engaged eight to carry my wife, eight for himself, and ten for the writer, with three for the baggage. Having instructed his catechists to look after his flock, and his servants to entertain the rest of our party, who were expected to arrive the same evening, we were ready to start, and the kabara commenced, the strife again being who should carry my wife; I decided that those who had come with us the whole way should be her bearers, and we started. I think the whole village's inhabitants were there to witness our departure, and they seemed very much distressed at seeing their pastor leave them. I believe he is beloved by all who know him, natives, French, and Creoles, as much as his own countrymen.

It was about noon when we got away, and started at a good pace. Mr C. said he thought the distance we had to travel was estimated at forty-five miles. We travelled through magnificent scenery, of which I could not attempt to give a proper description: often through groves of orange trees, forests of large and splendid timber, on the banks of rivers and lakes, with beautiful green foliage overhanging, and as before, sometimes on the beach. I have seen a little of Asia, different parts of India, Ceylon, the Malay Peninsula, Java, China, Japan, Australia, and New Zealand, but all these countries are as a wilderness compared to the beautiful scenery of Madagascar. Passing through one of the villages, my wife as usual was in advance. The bearers put her down, and when we got up to the place there she was sitting with a large and wondering crowd around her. We would not allow our bearers to stop, dreading the long kabara that must ensue before getting away again. We passed through, expecting her bearers would immediately follow − but not so. When we got through the village there was no appearance of them coming. We stopped for them to get up to us, and I determined to put a stop to anything of that kind occurring again. They had often set her down before, but on this occasion they had behaved badly. I was ready to receive them when they came with the stout stick that was my constant companion, to help along my weak side; they saw my intention, and setting down the chair quickly, I only got a stroke at one or two of them, when all the rest bolted. Mr Campbell called them back, and when they came with bowed heads for their share of the punishment, it was too much – I could not inflict it: but at my request Mr Campbell informed them that it would be in store for them if they ever run off again with my wife out of sight; and for the rest of the journey they must keep close company. They attended well to these instructions. After that I was never left so much in the rear again.

The day was excessively hot, and we did not object to the bearers having a rest beside a stream, where there were no huts, to rest and cool themselves. A little before sunset we came to a village, where they placed us all down beside the rest-house or hut. Mr C. requested them to go on to the next village, but all to no purpose. They were determined to go no further that night, but after promising faithfully that they would take us to Tamatave the next day, he gave them money to get food and to buy a couple of chickens for our use. One of them that had often travelled with Mr C. before, whom he knew could cook, did so for us on this occasion. Our friend had a very large amount of patience, but it was sorely taxed by the bearers. He said he had given them twice the amount they should have had, and still they annoyed him to get more. At length I saw that his patience was exhausted, and he looked round for something to drive them away. I said, "Stop, Mr Campbell, if there is anything in that line to be done, allow me to operate". I introduced my stout companion to their notice, and off they went, almost like magic, disappearing by jumping into the surrounding huts. The great wonder to me was how he could use so much patient forbearance with them; at all events my stout companion put an end to their kabara for that night. The female had trotted along this journey very well.

Mr C. estimated that we had travelled about eighteen miles on our way; but the circuitous routes we made must have added several more miles to our journey. It was a mystery to me how they found their way through the forests and jungle, for it was seldom we could see a beaten track.

We took our dinner, native fashion, and used mostly the native service. Our bearers came again in a more respectful manner to arrange for the next day's journey, promising to start when the moon rose, which would be about three o'clock next morning. We then put up the door of our hut. Mr C. read a chapter in his Bible, offered up evening prayer, and then prepared to rest.

The servant had put up our curtain, which she always did in the best part of the hut, being opposite the doorways, where we could get a little air. Mr. C. had a hammock that he had procured, to have with him on his journeys to sleep in, instead of sleeping on dirty mats. I slung it up for him for the first time. We had all a very hearty laugh at his fruitless attempts to get into it. At length I gave him a lesson in the art; but worse still, he got in on one side and tumbled out at the other. Eventually, I assisted him in.

April 15th. We were up and astir early, and after morning prayer, our bearers were ready at the appointed time, and after the kabara we started off. The morning was fine and clear, and it was much more pleasant travelling than during the heat of the day, if it had not been for the risk of a breakdown. The moon being far on the wane, the light was not very good, and the leaders often stumbled, through their feet becoming entangled in the undergrowth. We had not proceeded very far until we came to a deep declivity, where, for our own personal safety, we left our carriages and scrambled down. Soon after we got on the beach, where travelling was much safer, but the sand made it much more laborious for the bearers; yet it was not always safe along the beach, for our rev friend informed us that he was once so travelling past where the surf had banked up a river, when it burst the bank and nearly swept them all into the sea. We crossed one river, and at half-past 10 a.m. we reached a little miserable village, where we stopped to breakfast. The bearers took a very long time to finish their meal. When spoken to about losing so much time, the only satisfactory reply that Mr C. could get was that they would surely take us to Tamatave.

The same evening, I felt very anxious, for my wife was ill and breaking down. We went many times to get them to start. At length a visitor got into their midst that made them get quickly out of his way. It was a large snake, with open mouth, that caused them to move, and although he introduced himself so unceremoniously into their company, not one of them attempted to molest him for the insult, but laughing, got quickly out of his way. Mr C. and myself destroyed it, and after a kabara, we got started off again. During their disputes, and on the journey, they often used a word that I thought sounded English, Pakenham. Our rev friend explained that it was the name of H.B.M. representative in Madagascar, who was a very John Bull in proportions, and had always sixteen bearers when he travelled.

We had started off at a good pace. They seemed determined to bring us to the end of our journey according to promise. About 3 p.m. we came to another large and noble river, where there was some large canoes for hire to cross over. We all got in one of the largest, with a few bearers to paddle; the rest of the bearers in others. When about half way across, my wife became very ill, I dare not move to her assistance, for the very slightest move everyone in the canoe knew of, and the caution was given to sit still. Mr C. was urging the bearers to pull quick, explaining the reason for such exertion; indeed, they might easily see for themselves, for she looked like a corpse. When spoken to, one of the bearers talked a great deal. I asked our friend if he was giving him insolence. He replied, that he was using very insolent laguage. Through being so kindly treated, they began to take liberties, and were doing pretty much as they pleased. Before we had reached the other side, I was glad to hear my wife say she was much better, and was not sorry to hear that this was the last river we had to cross. As soon as we landed, I made my stout companion acquainted with the insolent bearer's back. He ran into the river, and all the rest [retreated] to a respectable distance. Mr C. called him back and explained why my stick hurt him. He admitted that he deserved the punishment.

We had made up our mind to stop at the village on the river bank, through my wife's illness, but feeling much better when we landed, she preferred proceeding. The force of my stick on the insolent bearer had a striking effect on the whole of them.

As previously, I was always left in the rear, but afterwards, my difficulty was to keep them from running me out of sight of the rest. This day's journey the female felt severely; during the morning my wife helped her along by taking hold of her hand, the bearers not allowing that she should hold on [to] the chair. It was a great relief to know we had finished the canoe travelling, yet we crossed some splendid rivers, in many of which there was room, and I believe anchorage, for all the British fleet, if the surf would only leave a navigable entrance to get into them. It almost seems wrong that such a rich and beautiful country should be left in the keeping of such miserable, indolent creatures. I was informed that the island was rich in minerals, and saw myself heaps of lead ore lying on the river banks, as clean as when washed for shipment at the mines.

From the last river we crossed, to Tamatave, appeared to be the most sterile and uninteresting part of our journey. We had sight of Tamatave as the sun was setting, some three miles off, at which time we also could see that our bearers had greatly augmented. We stopped on a grassy plain to check the list of names of our bearers. They said that all the increased force were engaged by themselves to assist, and that they would pay them. I omitted to remark on their wanton destruction of timber; we passed through a large forest, some two miles long, and perfectly level, where noble trees had been growing, some of them splendid hardwood. They had all been fired, and thousands burned to the stump, to grow rice among them.

Soon after numbering our force, we could see the spire of the little English church, and the dome of the Roman Catholic chapel, and the town altogether looked rather imposing in the distance; but on nearer approach, we were disappointed. Having heard so much about Tamatave from both Europeans and natives, as being the great maritime emporium of Madagascar, we did expect to find a much more respectable town than it turned out to be. We cannot boast of having seen all the town, but if the principal street or thoroughfare, where the Europeans reside, forms any criterion, we did not miss any grand sight in not visiting the native portion; for it would surely be in deep mourning. In the principal thoroughfare, each house was built inside a compound, according to a proprietor's idea of tropical architecture. The inhabitants of the main street, I should think, paid no scavenger rate, for it remained as nature had left it – sand. However, such as the town was, we were very glad to get to it, and very kindly indeed were we received by every European in the place. Our rev friend conducted us to the house of Messrs Proctor Brothers, where we arrived after dark, and just in time for dinner. After dinner, [we met] Mr Plant, an agent for Lloyds, and the Rev Chiswell, S.V.G., minister of the little church; our rev friend Campbell belonged to the Church Missionary Society.

The whole of the party escorted us to the house that Mr Creaux, the British vice-consul, had very thoughtfully provided for us. The house, I was told, belonged to the Princess Juliett, sister-in-law to Mr Edward Liger, our very kind friend at Mahila. The Princess had granted the use of it free during our stay. There was also another house in the compound for the crew. The poor native female that Mr Liger had sent with us to attend my wife, during the last part of our journey, had fairly broken down, footsore and tired out. Some of the bearers had to help her along, and she did not arrive until more than an hour after us. Our friends soon took leave, and we retired to rest; but not so soon to sleep, for our old enemy the surf was close to, keeping up its constant roar.

April 16th. The good old adage, of "Early to bed and early to rise", seems to be well kept up at this place, and throughout Madagascar, by the European community. We rose early, but not too soon; for about 6 a.m. J. E. Creaux, Esq., the British vice-consul, called, and he was exceedingly kind to us. He arranged that we should fare at the Messrs Proctor's table. Before Mr Creaux left, our rev friends Campbell and Chiswell, and very shortly all our friends of the evening before, came in. We had got into the midst of kind friends. During the day, one of the Sisters of Mercy, a French lady, called upon us. She brought my wife some useful little presents, and assisted very much in getting clothes made; and calling every day to enquire after her health, and to know if there was anything more she could do or get done for her. Old Captain Parsons, and the American consul, were kind; in fact, every one was kind to us. We shall never forget all the kindness we received. H.B.M. consul, Pakenham, was not on the island; he had gone to Bourbon to stop during the wet or sickly season at Madagascar, and had not returned up to the time of our departure from Tamatave.

During the afternoon, our very worthy friend, the British vice-consul, called, requesting me to accompany him to the fort; the Rev Campbell was also to be of our party. We were to pay our respects to the governor, whether it was a matter of etiquette or precaution, I know not, nor did I enquire. We got in our carriages, having each four bearers. The distance being short, we did not require relays. We arrived at the fort entrance about 4 p.m., passed through the first gate, and there was a guard to stop our further advance, until we had sent our names to their excellencies; for this important fortress and position boasted two governors, first and second. We had not long to wait, when a servant came with the requisite permission for us to advance into the dirty enclosed space; it may not always be in such a neglected condition, but like all who dwelt within it, might have been in mourning at this particular time. However, there was some attempt at elevation, for up to this time, we had not seen a house with a staircase or floor above, except one, that was under repair, belonging to Mr Liger at Mahila. We were conducted up a narrow, dark, rickety staircase, and ushered into the presence of both their excellencies, who, as at all other places, were sitting on a mat on the floor, in deep mourning, with their staff in a line beside them. Their excellencies rose at our entrance, shook hands, and greeted us very kindly. The first governor could speak a little English. We remained a short time, took leave, and returned to the town. We dined between 6 and 7, returned to our house, and went early to bed.

April 17th. We rose early, about 6 a.m. Our very excellent and kind friend, the vice-consul, paid his morning call, and shortly after our rev friends Campbell and Chiswell, and the Messrs Proctors, and all our kind friends; the governors sent a present of rice, fowls, and a goose. About sunset, Stout A.B., one of our party of the first boat, arrived, brought in a chair. He informed me that the remainder of our party he had left at the village, on the bank of the last river we had crossed. They had all been stricken down with fever. I enquired after the other party of the second boat. He said they had not heard anything concerning them. He was well cared for, and arrangements were made for bringing in the remainder of the party in chairs the following morning.

April 18th. Chairs had been sent early, and before noon the remainder of the party were brought in, all being more or less bad with fever. They were all lodged and well cared for. I spoke to the vice-consul about the other party, that it was very requisite a European should go to look after them and get them along, they having been equal to four days in advance of us on the journey, and no news yet heard of them. He promised that one should be sent to search for the party the same evening.

April 19th, Sunday. We attended the little church. The Rev Chiswell conducted the service. News arrived from Mr Plant that he had heard of the whereabout of the missing boat's crew. Nothing further of importance occurred, until April 24th, letters were received from Mr Plant, that he and the men might be expected to reach Tamatave on the 25th or 26th. During these last few days there was a great deal of heavy rain, and sometimes thunder and lightning, which must have been very severe on the seamen travelling. Mr Plant reported in his despatch that they were conducting themselves very badly. He advised the vice-consul to engage an empty house for them, to fasten them in, and throw their food through the window. This news very much alarmed the English residents of their coming, fearing they would disturb the peace of the town.

April 26th, Sunday. We attended the little church, thc Rev Thomas Campbell conducted the service, and preached a very impressive sermon. Madagascar is a good field for missionary labour. The natives have no religion of their own; and now, since England has a treaty with the country, no Jezebel Queen will dare again to massacre the Christian community with impunity, as before has happened. The Roman Catholics appear to make great progress there; they have a large school at Tamatave, which the Sisters of Mercy conduct. Besides educating the children, they teach them to sew, and other useful household work. The Sisters are also very much liked by the European inhabitants, for they are found very useful in sickness; some of them being skilled in medicine. The only English residents are those whom I have already mentioned.

This day we had the honour of breakfasting with the Princess Juliett, and her sister, Madame Liger, at the residence of J. E. Creaux, Esq., British vice-consul. During the day, Mr Plant returned home, and said the men would arrive next morning.

April 27th. The men did not arrive, but we heard during the day that they had arrived on the nearest bank of the last river, and were stopping in the village there.

April 28th. At an early hour, chairs and bearers were sent, and the chief mate went to escort them. They arrived shortly after noon. The peaceable inhabitants had little need to fear them committing a breach of the peace; and whatever fears they had were soon turned to pity, when they saw the poor, miserable looking, fever-stricken sailors. I never saw a more emaciated, sickly set of men in my life. The worthy vice-consul paid them great attention, and ordered them wine or any other nourishment that could be procured to do them good. Our rev friends, Campbell and Chiswell, were most assiduous in their attention to them. All the Englishmen in the place were ready to do their utmost for them. Two of them were very low.

April 29th. At 3 a.m. Daniel Roberts, the cook, expired, and was the same day interred in the Christian burial ground. The vice-consul arranged that we of the first boat should go as passengers in the *Caprice*, a regular trader to Mauritius, or more commonly called a bullocker. At my request it was arranged that the two boys, Radcliffe and Clarke, should be allowed in the cabin. They were both very weak and emaciated. I feared they would scarcely rally through the effects of the fever. All the party went on board on this evening, except my wife and myself, who were to go on board early the following morning.

Our rev friend, Campbell, promised us that the first time he made a journey to Mahila, he would read the burial service over our dear son's remains, and place a better inscription over the grave. At 7 p.m. Edward Giffen, A.B. expired.

April 30th. At 6 a.m. we were escorted to the beach by our very kind friends, being the whole British community of Tamatave. The boat was lying at the beach. All our kind friends bade us farewell; and we left Madagascar.

And here my narrative should have ended, had we not been doomed to suffer again, and were brought almost to the brink of death in a fearful cyclone. We got on board the bullocker about 7 a.m. All on board were very kind to us. The captain gave up his own berth to us. The perfume was anything but pleasant. Immediately after we got on board, the captain looked round, and said there was too much surf and sea on for us to sail. Most of the bullocks were only shipped the day before; had not yet got their sea legs under them; or, more properly speaking, were not sufficiently used to the motion of the vessel; and if taken outside, a great many might fall down and get killed. However, when we got on board, they were having a good lesson at getting their sea legs under them, for the vessel was rolling very much in this good harbour of Tamatave. It was an awful place to be called a harbour, every way you looked there was our old enemy the surf, breaking, roaring, and foaming over the reefs, that formed what was called the harbour. We were sorry to have to stop any time so near our old enemy, but stop we must.

The bullockers, I believe, are all old, condemned merchant vessels at Mauritius. The good old barque *Caprice* was one of this class of vessels, and I should think about 400 tons register; she was French built, and I have no doubt a very good one in her younger days. She had, I was told, 240 bullocks on board, 90 on the upper or main deck, and the remainder between decks. The bullocks on the main deck were penned in, about fifteen in each pen; and there was a large open space amidships, right fore and aft, for ventilation to those that were below; and above was a spar deck, made from old spars and planks. The ship was worked on the spar deck, the warps and lumber were also carried there. The captain soon after he decided not to sail was going on shore. He invited my wife and me to go along with him, but we declined troubling our kind friends any more; and preferred remaining on board to be rocked in the dirty cradle of the deep. The captain could speak very little English; the mate could speak it pretty well; the second mate none at all.

I wished to know all the art and manner of bullock carrying, and commenced to make enquiries of the mate. In the lower hold was carried the water and hay, what in England we would have called very common straw. The bullocks got neither water or hay the first three days; it was supposed that they carried enough moisture with them from the shore, including the salt water they had to swallow going through the surf, to satisfy them for that length of time. On the fourth day they got a small allowance. I enquired particularly where they kept the hatches, or other apparatus for covering up the large openings fore and aft in the deck, in the event of meeting with bad weather. To my great astonishment, he told me they had nothing of the sort; but he added, the bad weather is now all past for this season. I hoped so, and thought tomorrow will be the first of May. It ought to be past. All we seafaring community are ready to give our opinions, either from hearsay, experience, or books, concerning seasons, winds, and weather; yet, after all, how little do we erring mortals know!

Before we took dinner, I had learned all I wished of bullockers in general, and of the *Caprice* in particular, a great deal more than I liked. She had a motley crew of Creoles and Malagasis, bad gear, bad sails, and in my opinion she was not seaworthy. The only thing in our favour was, that she was in fine light trim. I did not like the craft. But what was to be done? Our only way of getting from Madagascar was by the bullockers, and the good ship *Caprice* was considered one of the best of the fleet that was in the trade. These vessels do not sail during the stormy or hurricane season. It being the month of May when we were making our passage, was the only consolation. After a quiet dinner, we went to bed, but not so soon to sleep. My wife was very weak; yet we were the only two that escaped an attack of fever. The two boys were very low.

May 1st. We were up early, after a very restless night, or I might say, we were up most of the night; for, with the loud roaring of the surf, the rolling of the ship, steam and foul odours from the bullocks, and swarms of savage mosquitoes, it was impossible to sleep. The captain came on board soon after sun-rise. He looked round, and said it was too rough outside for the bullocks; and sailing was again given up for the day. We had a present sent on board of rice, fowls, a goose, and two pieces of calico, from their excellencies, the two governors. We sent acknowledgment by letter. It will be seen that the governors and all the officials, wherever we found them, were very liberal, and indeed all the officials of the government are so, for we were well informed that none of them receive any pay from their government for official services. All the remuneration they receive is the honour. We had several opportunities of going on shore, but declined. During the day the vessel was moved into a clearer berth, for we had been lying very convenient to a reef. We had two Limas on board, that had been presented by our kind friends to my wife. These animals some people call Malagasi cats. I never saw of them before, and was told that they were peculiar to Madagascar. I observed that the crew looked as if they did not like them, but had no idea that they had any superstitious dread of the animals. The day passed over very tediously, and the following night worse.

May 2nd. Soon after daylight, the captain again pronounced the weather too rough for the bullocks to go to sea. This day was a repetition of the two days previous, and to us it was awfully miserable, to be lying so near the surf.

May 3rd, Sunday. At an early hour, the captain came on board, and said he would sail. Miserable as it was to us lying there, we should very much have liked him to put it off until the next day, remembering how unfortunate our last Sunday sailing had been; but we had no voice in the matter, being merely passengers. So, away we went past the reefs and surf, and glad we were when we got clear of our enemy's awful noise. The wind was a brisk breeze from the south, and the weather cloudy. The bullocks seemed to stand it well, for stand they must; if any of them attempted to lie down, the men on watch beat them until they got up again. During the day they were served with some water and hay.

May 4th. Strong breeze from the southward, and cloudy weather. Bullocks are better sailors than I thought they would have been. There was nothing of importance occurred except splitting some of the sails, and carrying away the gear, which did not require much force of wind to effect it.

May 5th. We had a strong breeze from the southward, and cloudy weather. The bullocks were standing well, but there was two deaths among them, the carcasses were cast into the sea. There was no attempt made to clean, and the reader may imagine how foul an atmosphere we had to breathe.

May 6th. We had a brisk breeze from S.W., and gloomy weather. I did not at all like the appearance of the weather. The barometer, like nearly everything else on board, was French, and I could not read it, but could see, by the position of the mercury, that it was rather low; but still there was the thought, it is the month of May. The fall in the barometer may be for rain.

May 7th. Commenced a moderate breeze from S.S.W., and gloomy. I did not like the appearance of the weather, although it was the month of May. I spoke to the captain, explaining as well as I could my opinion of things in general, and pointed to the barometer. He admitted it was very low, but said, "Hurricane no month May". During the evening, the wind decreased to a very moderate breeze, but the appearance of the weather was worse, and the barometer still falling. I spoke again to the captain, and advised that we should run northward, and try to avoid the coming storm. He said, "If it were the stormy season, he would do so, but month of May no hurricane". We retired, but not to sleep, I was going about most of the night. The barometer still falling.

May 8th. At 1 a.m. I went up on the poop. It was the chief mate's watch. He and my late chief were having a long talk, their bodies being placed in a very comfortable position. The wind at the time was a very moderate breeze from the westward; but the weather looked very bad. I asked the mate of the ship where the captain was. He replied that he was in bed. I asked if he knew how low the barometer was. He said, it was no lower than the evening before. I said, be the barometer how it would, the weather looked very bad, and it was full time that he was on deck, attending to his duty. He took no notice of my expressions, but quietly resumed the conversation. I suppose, thinking it was the month of May, and being in the vicinity of where he was born, [he] thought he knew more about the weather than I did. I went below; my wife enquired how I thought the weather looked. I said that it looked very bad, and it would, before long, burst upon us; and related the manner in which I was insulted by the mate of the ship. She asked me if I would call the captain; I said I would not. He had no right to be asleep at such a time, and if alone, he might wake to find his masts alongside. She said, "I will call him", and had him out quick. I pointed to him the barometer, and the appearance of the weather, and made him understand that I thought it was full time for him to prepare his ship for the worst. He went on deck, and commenced taking in the small sails, for the old ship had all possible sail set. Our brave captain was gone none too soon in reducing his canvas, for, by the time he had got in the small sails, the wind commenced to pipe, and he still reduced. At daybreak, the wind was rapidly increasing. As soon as we had daylight, although the crew did not understand English, I easily made them understand the danger of the great openings in the deck. While the captain was commanding on the poop, I took the liberty of giving orders on the main deck, in laying spars and planks across the openings, and sails to cover over at hand.

At 9 a.m. the main topsail was taken in, the old ship was then running under the lower fore topsail. I had often to go in and see my wife; indeed, I told her there was very little hope, and we both wished we had gone with our children in the sea. We prayed together, supposing it would be the last time; after which, I went on deck to see that the men were standing by the rails, ready to cover up the openings. The lightning flashed, and thunder roared, the fore topsail burst into shreds. I called out to the men to cover up, they attended to my order, assisted myself, and told them that if the ship broached to before these openings were secured, and shipped one sea, we would all be lost. The covering up was death to all the bullocks below. I told my wife there was again a little hope. So much thunder and lightning denoted the storm to be of the cyclone character; it would not last long. At this time the steward came for the Limas, saying the captain wanted to destroy them; we did not share in their superstition, and were not prepared to give them up; but he said the sailors will do no more until they are killed. Then I said, "Take them". I went to see what they did with the Limas. The second mate took them, swung each three times round his head, then dashed them with all his strength on the deck, and threw them into the sea. The ship soon after broached to on the starboard tack, which was the proper tack for our position; but she shipped a large quantity of water. The ship was laying very badly along. The captain and crew seemed to have lost all presence of mind, and left the poor old ship to her fate. I and my late chief mate went on the poop, and for the time being took charge, and [the] whole of the crew willingly obeying my orders; braced the yards, got relieving tackles on the rudder-head, and a storm sail in the mizen rigging, to keep [the] ship's head to wind, means that they evidently had never before seen adopted. It was a very severe cyclone, and the old ship laboured and strained heavily. The captain and his officers were often slipping down into the cabin, and were drinking deep; the effect of which was soon apparent upon them; I suppose their idea was, to die gloriously drunk. My wife found an opportunity of speaking to the steward, telling him not to let them have any more, or the ship would be lost. He acted on this advice, and told them all the strong drink was broken and lost. We got the ship trimmed about noon, when I urged the captain to have the deckload of bullocks thrown overboard, many of them at that time being almost dead, with broken limbs, and lying in heaps, gored by falling upon each other, and altogether in a sad state. He agreed, and part of the crew were told off for that duty, the remainder working the pumps, for there was a great deal of water in the ship.

It was a fearful afternoon, blowing very hard, vivid flashes of lightning, peals of thunder, and a deluge of rain, but in this phenomena was our hope, that it would not last so long as the dreaded hurricane. Before sunset, the atmosphere began to break, and it was apparent that the heaviest of the storm was past. The old ship was in a most deplorable state, the hurricane or spar deck had given way, and all fallen in. The groans of the bullocks below, that were dying of suffocation, and otherwise, the filth, the stench, the spars flying about, expecting every moment that the whole of her spars would go over the side. She had eased herself of some of the small spars. The old ship looked an awful wreck. Before dark, half the deck load of bullocks was thrown overboard, and it was impossible to get at any more, through the spar deck that had fallen having blocked them up. The bullocks below did not groan very long, their noise ended soon after dark.

But the awful effluvias that arose were unbearable in the cabin, where all was in a heterogenous mass. From the setting of the sun, the weather gradually moderated, and very glad we were to find it so, for the old ship would not have stood much more. As it was, she laboured and strained heavily all night, and was making a great deal of water. Both pumps were constantly going, and still I think the water was gaining. To breathe in the cabin doorway was a difficulty, and every moment the foul odours were increasing. At midnight, the wind was north, and all the while moderating. At daybreak, the wind was N.E. As soon as possible I got my wife up on the poop, the only place where it was possible to get a little sweet air. After a little consultation, it was decided to let the old ship run; our course being to the S.W, but it was requisite to find sails to run with; the old fore topmast staysail, that had been in the mizen rigging, was taken down to bend, in place of one that had been blown to pieces. The foresail had been saved by furling it in time. These two sails were set, and the old ship put before the wind. Orders were then given to loose and set the lower main topsail, but when they went aloft for that purpose, [they] found the main topmast badly sprung in the doublings; secured it with a chain, what seamen call a Spanish cap, and afterwards set the sail.

May 9th. Some time after daylight, the weather cleared off a little, and we were thankful to the Almighty when the sun once more shone out upon us. The old ship by daylight did look a miserable wreck. Of the bullocks that remained on deck, some were dead and some dying, with the wreck of the spar deck lying upon them, and only some fourteen or sixteen of the whole cargo were saved alive. There was still a great deal of water in the ship, and both pumps were constantly going. We had good hopes again, if she could only be cleared of the water that was in her. At the best, our living on board the bullocker was very coarse; but during the storm the cookhouse and apparatus were smashed, and strewn amongst the debris on deck, so that cooking operations were entirely suspended; but they got some temporary arrangement, and by noon-day we had some breakfast prepared for us. We took ours on deck, for the stench was unbearable below; indeed, we had to remain all our time on the poop, until we arrived at Mauritius. At noon, the old ship was bounding on her way with all possible sail set; and, by observation, we were eighty miles distant from that island. During the afternoon, the crew were employed at the pumps, and getting the dead bullocks overboard. From the time the hatches were opened, it is impossible to describe the awful stench. The crew of the bullocker no doubt are inured to filth and stench, but it was even too much for them, for several had to part with their breakfast much quicker than they liked. When darkness set in, the hatches were covered up, which was a little relief, but still it was unbearable in the cabin. During the evening the ship was pumped dry, which was a great relief to our minds. At 11 p.m. we sighted the light on the island. The pumps were regularly attended during the night. Midnight, the wind decreased to a light breeze from the eastward.

May 10th. Daylight, we sighted the land, which gladdened our hearts; for the old ship was very much disabled, and she had only two miserable small and old boats. With the daylight, the extreme stench was again opened to us by uncovering the hatches to get more of the dead carcasses overboard. A little before noon the hatches were covered up again, and about noon we anchored in the roads outside Port Louis. Soon after we had anchored, a pilot came alongside. I suppose he thought the old ship smelled too strong to be taken into port, for he would not come on board. However, the state of the ship was reported to him in a modified form. We also reported ourselves being on board, and wished to get out of the filth and stench as soon as possible. He promised to make the report, and immediately left. Soon afterwards, we had a heavy fall of rain, which lasted about one hour. The old awning we had spread, saved us very little from its force, yet it was more pleasant to get wet than endure the foul odours below.

About 2 p.m. the health visit came alongside. The doctor made a very short visit, no doubt feeling that the foul atmosphere on board the old ship was neither wholesome nor agreeable. When leaving, he made my wife and me the offer of a passage on shore with him, which we very gladly and thankfully accepted. While we were passing onshore, the harbour master had sent a small tug to convey us. They took all that was left of my late crew. On landing, Mr Morgan, the harbour master, and other officials, gave us a very kindly welcome to their port, and sympathised with us in our bereavement and distress. While speaking to them, the owner of the *Caprice* and the bullocks came up, asking me if I did not think the bullocks might have been saved. Saying, he thought the captain had too soon sealed their fate, and I suppose thinking, at the same time, that the bullocks had as much, if not more right than us to live. Considering they were his property, and the ship his own, I replied, that the only fault I could find with the captain was, that he spared the bullocks' lives too long, thereby very greatly endangering our own lives. He then very quickly made his exit. Mr Morgan recommended us to put up at the sailors' home; where he said we would get apartments, and fare better than at any hotel in the place. He sent a person as our guide to that institution, where we arrived about 4 p.m. The superintendent, a British subject, and old shipmaster, received us very coolly, and long hesitated to accommodate us; but said we had better try some of the hotels. We told him we were perfect strangers, and who it was that did recommend us. But still he hesitated, saying, he had no apartments for us; but, after a long consideration, he sent us to look at a sleeping apartment. It was anything but

grand, nor had it any appearance of respectability; yet on the whole it was more comfortable than any we had occupied for some time.

We felt the cool reception very acutely, for up to that time there was no European
we had met with, from the time we landed on the beach at Madagascar, but treated us
with the greatest kindness; but here was our own countryman, who had been long of
the same profession, well known to me by sight, although fully expecting to pay for our
living, which he knew yet treated us with such incivility. I am happy to say that no other
European in the port treated us but with the greatest kindness, and even the worthy
superintendent, I think, afterwards regretted the manner in which he received us, and
both he and his good lady treated us very kindly; and we fared right well with them in
the cabin of the sailors' home.

We had scarcely got accepted to be put up, when the officers and crew that had
come in the *Caprice* with us, arrived at the establishment. There was no difficulty about
their reception, for they required no private apartment, but they were all weak and ill,
except the chief mate. The old *Caprice* was ordered into quarantine, until she should be
well and properly cleaned out, which I think was a very wise precaution, for the stench
from her, I think, was enough to cause infectious disease in the port, of which there was
no need, for plenty of fever existed there without.

It is impossible that I could speak too highly of the great kindness we received from
Mr Morgan before named, and all the port officials.

13th May. The second mate and Stout A.B., went into hospital this day. I called on
Messrs Blythe Brothers, merchants, presenting a letter of introduction from the worthy
British vice-consul at Tamatave. These gentlemen were exceedingly kind, and rendered
me very great service in settling my affairs.

May 12th. I was informed that there would be an inquiry by the Marine Board the
following day into the circumstances of the loss of the ship *Serica*.

May 13th. I and my officers were in attendance, and examined as to the cause of the
loss of our ill-fated ship. The Board did not require much information concerning the
violence of the storm, they having felt its full fury on the island, where a large amount
of damage was done; houses unroofed and blown down, an iron railway bridge blown
off its columns, the wreck of which I saw lying in the valley; an iron church, we were
told, was turned over; of some seventy or eighty ships lying moored in the harbour,
some became total wrecks, many cut away their masts, and all except two or three were
more or less damaged. It was said to be the heaviest storm that had occurred during the

memory of the oldest inhabitant at Mauritius, so that the Board knew well what our unfortunate ship had to encounter when that awful storm came down upon us. What they wished to know was how we managed her during such a storm. Their report was as follows:-

"It appears from the evidence of the witnesses, that on the *Serica* leaving Liverpool, she was tight, staunch, and sea-worthy, and had undergone a partial repair, having been carefully caulked and re-coppered whilst in port, and that she was moderately laden. She appears to have had a prosperous voyage up to 11th March, when it came on to blow hard from the E.S.E. On the morning of the 12th, sail was shortened, the ship wore round, and hove to on the port tack, under a close reefed main topsail. The barometers being steady all that day at 29.80. On the gale increasing from the same point, the royal yards were sent down and all other top hamper, extra lashings were put on the boats, and the sails made well fast to the yards. Double relieving tackles were put on the rudder head, in fact, every precaution appears to have been taken that an experienced commander could do for the safety of his vessel.

"At 6 a.m. on the 13th, the gusts becoming very heavy, the main topsail was clued up, tarpaulins and hammocks were then made fast in the mizen rigging, for the purpose of keeping the ship's head to wind.

"At noon, the storm increasing, and the barometers rapidly falling to 28.60, the rudder having become useless, after the breaking of the iron band which secured the rudder head, the vessel falling off and becoming unmanageable, the foremast was cut away, the main and mizen soon followed it. After cutting away the masts, the vessel, it appears, sprung a serious leak, that at once necessitated the continued use of both pumps. A butt must have been started by the bumping of the spars alongside, before the wreck could be got clear of the vessel. The cargo was hove overboard, as well as it could be got at from a scuttle in the cabin. The rudder went away in spite of all the efforts that were made to save it.

"The water was now gaining on the pumps, and it appeared clear to all on board, the vessel would soon founder. It was then, and only then, that a raft was made, and the boats got out for the purpose of saving life. Too much cannot be said of the cool, gallant, and seamanlike conduct of Captain C−, the commander, throughout the whole of this trying time.

"The Board are sorry they cannot say the same of the crew, who at the last allowed their fears to overcome that steady, cool obedience which should ever distinguish the British sailor in the hour of danger. The Board are therefore unanimously of [the] opinion, that the abandonment of the *Serica* was necessary, and that the master and officers only adopted that course when all chance of saving the property ceased, and that no blame whatsoever can be attached to them for the loss of the vessel".

I do not wonder at our friends not being able to understand the reports of the catastrophe, for it is made to appear that we left the ship in our frail boats at the height of the storm. At such a time as we then had, I do not think any open boat could have lived.

May 17th. The remainder of the crew that was spared arrived on board the *Admiral*, another of the bullockers; they escaped the cyclone, but were all very weak and ill, and looked very emaciated. One of them, Jeremiah Driscoll, went into hospital, the remainder of them were lodged in the sailors' home.

May 18th. I engaged a passage for myself and wife in the *Canopus*, of and for London. I entreated the shipping master to send the boys, Radcliffe and Clarke, as government passengers, in the same vessel, so that we might look after them. On the passage, they were both very ill. He readily agreed to the proposal, and arranged accordingly.

I settled with all my late crew, paying them by order on England, and on the 20th, we went on board the *Canopus*, an iron ship, and a very fine vessel. She was not half loaded, but was to sail with half a cargo. On the 22nd we sailed, and had exceedingly fine weather for the season round the Cape of Good Hope, which was very fortunate for us, for the good ship *Canopus* was not right about her rudder which made a great noise, and worked a great deal, but, unfortunately for us, she was a very slow ship.

The boy Radcliffe, after leaving, soon began to improve in health, but a sloughing ulcer formed on one of his legs, which would not yield to my treatment. After a long passage we arrived off St Helena, and, without anchoring, we took him on shore, and left him in hospital. Clarke remained very weak the whole passage, which was a very tedious one; so much so, that we were reduced to very hard fare; but that was not so bad as our great anxiety to see our children, having heard nothing concerning them from leaving home. We had a great deal of light and baffling winds and calms in the vicinity of the Azores. During the calms we had plenty of vessels for company, but as soon as a breeze sprung up, we were often left alone. On the 1st September we were in soundings.

On the morning of the 6th, we were near the Eddystone lighthouse. After leaving the boy Clarke in charge of one of the ship's officers, to see him safe away from London, and on his way home, we took passage in a pilot boat to Plymouth, where we arrived at 1 p.m. We had not a moment to lose in reaching the train, in which we could get through to Liverpool; we changed trains at Bristol, and arrived at Lime Street Station, Liverpool, on the 7th, at 3 a.m.

Sunday. We spent the day in our lodgings, without visiting any of our friends. On the 8th we took passage per steamer and arrived at Douglas, Isle of Man, and home the same evening, and were glad to find all our dear children in good health.

Since our arrival home, I wrote to the Board of Trade, making a representation of the very kind services of Mr Edward Liger to us in our great distress, wishing a government acknowledgment of his kindness; but up to the present time I have heard of no result, except through a friend at Tamatave, who wrote, stating that a copy of my letter had been sent to the British consul at Madagascar for confirmation. Mr Liger had a gold medal and decorations from the Emperor Napoleon, for similar services to French seamen. I have also received a letter from the Rev Thomas Campbell, stating that he had visited Mahila, and found that Mr Liger had our son's grave nicely railed in, and that he, Mr C., had fulfilled his promise of reading the burial service and placing a better inscription over his remains. Mr Liger further informed him that he had the beach watched long after we left, but no portion of our little boy or the seaman's remains were ever cast up.

Jeremiah Driscoll's wages were paid to the Board of Trade, the Board informing that he died on board another ship very shortly after leaving Mauritius, and the order was found amongst his effects.

Such was the end of our disastrous voyage. We returned home sadder and poorer than we left, and my poor wife's constitution very much broken down. Yet, thankful that the Almighty had spared us, after being so often at the brink of death, to return to our native land and family again.

Occasional words in [square brackets] have been inserted to clarify the meaning of the original text.

AFTERWORD

NO ONE, after the event, would ever be able to doubt Thomas Cubbin's account of the hurricane which sank the *Serica*, for its ferocity was reported around the world. Under the headline DREADFUL HURRICANE AT THE MAURITIUS, New Zealand's *Taranaki Herald* of 23rd May 1868 repeated a story which had previously appeared in Australia's *Sydney Herald*, in its turn translated from the French of the *Bulletin Commercial du Cerneen,* brought from Mauritius to Suez. Originally dated Port Louis, 18th March, it read:

> We have just undergone a great public misfortune; one of the most violent tempests ever known has swept over the colony. We have, like the Antilles, paid our tribute to those atmospheric convulsions which seem unable to spare any country on the globe.
>
> For many years past we have not experienced such a disaster. The effects of the cyclone are not yet known in all their complete details; but reports have been received by us from all the districts of the island, sufficiently numerous to enable us to give a tolerably definite idea of the precise nature of the catastrophe.

There follows an account of up to a quarter of the sugar cane crop in Mauritius being lost, the destruction of a Catholic chapel with the serious injury of one brother and the death of a pupil, the carrying away of all the roofs of buildings in the dock, 'and the covering of the soldiers' camp ... carried away by a waterspout to the distance of from 300 to 400 feet'. Water stood 'to a considerable depth' in the city's theatre, sugar stored in dock warehouses was ruined, seven ships were wrecked in the harbour, and twenty dead bodies were picked up in the streets. The *Bulletin* chose to highlight one particular episode:

> At Redout, his Excellency the Governor and Lady Barkly were seated in a room near a table, when Sir Henry suddenly rose, and, followed by Lady Barkly, went into another room to consult his barometer. Scarcely had both of them left the apartment, when a chimney, carried away by the wind, fell through part of the roof and smashed the very table and chairs at which his Excellency and Lady Barkly had taken refuge, under the impression that they would there be safe.

Thomas and Mary Cubbin returned to their home at Rose Hill in the Isle of Man on 8th September 1868, to find their four young daughters, Esther, Mary, Jane and Amy, well. But they were, as Thomas wrote, 'sadder and poorer than we left, and my poor wife's constitution very much broken down'.

He was reluctant even to see his friends, and must have shut himself away at home for much of the next year in order to concentrate on writing *The Wreck of the Serica*. In 1870 the memoir was published, the memorial tablet to Tom and James was erected at Kirk Braddan, and there was at least new life to bring some consolation. On 26th June 1870 Thomas and Mary carried their last child to Braddan for Parson Drury to baptise. She was given the names Serica Isabella.

Thomas was only forty-five when he lost the *Serica*, and he still had a sizeable family to support. Very soon after he got home he was approached by the widow of one of the previous owners to buy shares in the dandy-rigged *Ocean Gem,* built in Castletown in 1864 (a different *Ocean Gem*, very much smaller, from the one he sailed to China in 1861-3). She was registered in his name in 1868, and he owned her until 1875-7, during which he gradually sold his shares in the vessel to the Gale family of Port St Mary. As far as is known he never sailed her commercially himself. A Douglas man, Thomas Hampton, is registered as her master from 1869, and she was used as a coaster around the shores of the British Isles, venturing just once, in the summer of 1872, as far as Caen in Normandy.

In 1873 Thomas also bought a seventy-six ton schooner, the *Cassowary*, built at Port Hawkesbury, Nova Scotia, only two years before. He was registered as the *Cassowary's* master and owner for that year, brought her across the Atlantic from Halifax, and also sailed down into the Mediterranean as far as Tunis. From 1874 on, he employed a series of other masters to take her to sea – a Jerseyman, Thomas LeClercq of St Helier, then two Douglas men, William Drennan and Henry Kelly. He sold her again to Edward Martin of Castletown in 1876.

Already in 1873 there had been signs of strain in the Cubbin family's finances. On 17th May that year Thomas and Mary jointly signed a Deed of Conditional Bond and Security, making over their 'mansion house and estate' to the Isle of Man Banking Company in the sum of £1,500, with an undertaking to pay interest, charges and no less than £900 per annum in fire insurance. This deed was not cancelled until 30th September 1875, two days before the estate was sold to

Arthur Appleby Menzies as trustee for his father Robert Henry Menzies; both father and son were wealthy Liverpool estate agents. Just a few fields were held back, but the handsome sum of £2,040 which Thomas and Mary realised probably formed the bedrock of their family finances for the rest of their lives. It must have broken their hearts to let the house go; it had been their home for twelve years, and Thomas always seemed proud to describe himself as 'of Rose Hill'.

On 1st June 1875 he had led his eldest daughter Esther, by then twenty, to Kirk Braddan to be married by Parson Drury to twenty-four year old John Cubbon. Esther's new husband worked with his father and brother as 'Joseph Cubbon & Sons, saddle, harness, trunk and portmanteau manufacturers' in Douglas. The couple would in due course produce a family of ten children, though not all lived to adulthood. When John Cubbon died suddenly in 1915 the *Isle of Man Examiner* claimed that 'Cubbon's harness and saddlery were world-famous'. John also seems to have been quite a character:

> His was an extremely charming personality, as he possessed the faculty of making himself agreeable to all classes, while his manner was ever pleasant and he was tactful to a high degree ... Mr John Cubbon's mind became richly stored with lore of old Douglas, and it was ever a pleasure to him to retail incidents of which he had either personal knowledge or which had reached him the while he worked at the saddler's bench and listened to patriarchal narrations. And as Mr Cubbon was a most excellent raconteur, the yarns lost nothing in his telling of them.

Even in her husband's obituary Esther's illustrious parentage was noted, for she is described as 'the daughter of the late Capt. Thomas Cubbon [sic], of Rose Hill, Braddan. Capt. Cubbon, by the way, had one of the most exciting experiences which ever befell a master mariner, in connection with the loss of the ship *Serica,* while under his command. The vessel was wrecked, and for a long time Capt. Cubbon and his crew underwent terrible hardships in an open boat and on a desert island ere they were rescued'.

Esther's own children seem to have inherited their grandparents' adventurous ways. Of the six surviving at the time of John Cubbon's funeral, one son was living in China, another in Edmonton, Alberta, and one daughter in Cairo; today their descendants are spread out across the globe.

Thomas Cubbin's last ship, the Mary, *alias the* S.G.G. Thompson, *alias 'the pirate Alexandra', when she was seized in Liverpool. Thomas's seagoing career appears to have ended after an incident in which she ran aground.*

ILLUSTRATED LONDON NEWS, 9TH MAY 1863

By 1876 Thomas and Mary Cubbin and their younger daughters had left the Isle of Man and were living in a rented home in Liverpool, at 17 River Avon Street, Edgehill. By 2011 there was just one house left standing in River Avon Street, no. 19. The Cubbins' home next door would have been very similar – a modest place compared with Rose Hill.

PHOTO VALERIE COTTLE

But to return to Thomas and Mary and their other daughters; they all appear to have left the Island by 1876, because they are then recorded as living in Liverpool, at 17 River Avon Street, Edgehill. In the spring of that year Thomas had bought yet another vessel, the *S. G. G. Thompson*, which had formerly been called the *Mary*. But in fact his new ship had a still earlier name, the *Alexandra*, and a very intriguing history.

During the American Civil War all kinds of subterfuges were undertaken by Liverpool merchants for the benefit of the Confederate States, amongst them the building of unarmed vessels, easily armed once they had crossed the Atlantic, with a view to running the blockade imposed on the Southern states by the ships of the Northern Union. Britain was supposed to be neutral, but the blockade caused a cotton famine and mass unemployment in the factories of Lancashire so, initially at least, the Government turned a blind eye to such activities.

A Confederate naval officer, Commander James Dunwoody Bulloch, came to Liverpool at the beginning of the war and commissioned half a dozen fast steamships suitable for blockade running. His first contract was with the engineering firm of Fawcett, Preston & Co.; a second was signed with Laird's. The *Alexandra*, a prospective Confederate cruiser, was launched on 7th March 1863, but spotted by Federal spies as soon as she appeared in the dock at Toxteth. She was an unusually constructed vessel, and depositions were taken to the effect that if she was not already a gunboat, she could easily be fitted out as one. The case went to court on 22nd June, the Crown claiming that, contrary to the Foreign Enlistment Act, her owners Fawcett Preston had equipped the *Alexandra* so that she could be employed 'in the service of the Confederate States of America with intent to cruise and commit hostilities against the Republic of the United States of America'. Fawcett Preston were acquitted, but many months of legal tussling followed before the vessel was released. They opted to settle for compensation of £3,700, then sold the ship to one Henry Lafone (in fact another Confederate agent) who renamed her the *Mary*.

This, however, was not the end of the story. By December 1864 the *Mary* was in Nassau, where a 12-pounder gun – with the stamp 'Fawcett Preston & Co. 1862' – and cases of shells were found on board. Once more she was detained, and again freed, but by 1865 the Civil War was over and it was too late for her to be of any use to the Confederacy. She returned to England where her engine was removed; she then traded for several years as a barque, and later as a schooner, under the name *S. G. G. Thompson*.

Thomas Cubbin bought the *S. G. G. Thompson* in 1876 from J.E. Poole & Son of Hayle in Cornwall. He sailed her to Swansea, and from there set out for the Mediterranean on 25th May, arriving in Barcelona on 16th June and in Tarragona on 1st July; his voyage ended back in Liverpool on 23rd August. Between 22nd September and 16th December he took her down the coast of Portugal, still under the name *S. G. G. Thompson*, calling in at Oporto on 9th October and Lisbon on 2nd November. These seem almost to have been in the nature of practices for a much longer voyage. He registered the vessel in Liverpool, not surprisingly changing her name back to *Mary* in honour of the wife who had endured such tribulations with him. On 18th April 1877 he sailed again, the crew agreement this time outlining a proposed route 'to Rio Grande do Sul [in Brazil], or any port or places in South or North America, Atlantic Ocean, West Indies or Continent of Europe, and back to the United Kingdom – maximum twelve months'.

But the crew agreement and log for this voyage, held in the National Archives at Kew, is odd in that there is no report of the vessel either being lost or returning to England. There is a note at the end of Thomas's service record, also at Kew, which reads 'Error of judgement when the *Mary* 50263 stranded'. We do not know where this occurred, or indeed even if it happened on the same voyage. It was not serious enough to be entered in the notorious Black Book, which is now held at the National Maritime Museum. But it appears to have marked the end of Thomas's seagoing career. Perhaps despite not being a disciplinary matter, it may simply have put paid to his confidence in himself as a competent seaman. What we do know is that the *Mary* continued in his ownership until 1881, and that in that year she was registered not in Liverpool, but in Shanghai.

The circumstances and place of Thomas Cubbin's death were never reported in the Isle of Man, and no one has ever seemed to know what happened to him. Only a chance encounter via the internet solved the mystery. Early in 2011 the author was contacted from California by James Cubbon, a great-grandson of John and Esther Cubbon (family tree, page 130), so Thomas and Mary Cubbin's great-great-grandson. James was able to supply the information that the Cubbins' eldest daughter Esther had written in 1904 to Sir Robert Hart to ask if, as Inspector General of the Chinese Maritime Customs Service, he could give a job to her son John. There were few opportunities in the Isle of Man at that time (indeed her brother-in-law Joseph had been one of the tradesmen who petitioned for the winding up of the ruined Dumbell's Bank in 1901). A letter dated 18th December 1904 from Sir Robert Hart to his agent in England refers to Esther and Thomas as follows: 'Mrs. Cubbon is the daughter of Capt. Cubbon [sic] who died before taking up a Tide-surveyor's appointment at Chefoo after the wreck of the vessel – the 'Serica' I think...'

This was more than three decades after Thomas had lost the *Serica*, but it remained the vessel most closely associated with his name. A search by Robert Fyson at the Colindale Newspaper Library subsequently turned up his death notice in the *North China Herald* of 8th November 1881:

> At Chefoo on the 3rd Nov., T. Cubbins, late Master of the schooner *Mary*.

The 1901 Isle of Man census had already provided a clue to some at least of the Cubbin family having gone to live permanently in China. According to the census, living or staying in Douglas with John and Esther Cubbon was a nephew, named as Thomas C. Conner, who had been 'born in 1892 in China'. It is unclear whether Thomas, Mary, and their four younger daughters, Mary, Jane, Amy and Serica, had sailed out to China specifically for Thomas to take up this Customs appointment (it was a Tide-Surveyor's job to 'rummage' ships lying offshore from a port for contraband goods before they could be landed), or whether he was there already with the *Mary*, and the whole family decided to stay. Chefoo is the city now called Yantai, west of Weihai, on the peninsula of Shandong province, jutting out into the Yellow Sea towards Korea. According to James Cubbon, some of his relatives believed Thomas to have been buried in Shanghai; if this is true his body must have been taken there from Chefoo after he died.

He had made a will in Liverpool in 1876, and after his death Mary had the task of bringing it back first to England, and then to the Isle of Man, to obtain probate. The British consul in Chefoo, H.P. McClatchie, certified the document as being 'a true copy of the Will of the late Thomas Cubbin deceased' on 28th

The Bund at Shanghai, with clippers and junks on the Huangpu River, by an unknown Chinese artist. Thomas and Mary Cubbin knew Shanghai well. It is believed that Thomas was buried in the city after his death at Chefoo in 1881, and Mary died here five years later. Their bodies were probably buried together in one of Shanghai's Christian cemeteries, but it is very unlikely that the graves survive.

November 1881, but it was May 1883 before probate was finally granted in Douglas and the assets could be distributed. In the will Thomas directed the disposal of his Manx-registered vessels *Cassowary* and *Ocean Gem*, but in the event they had both been sold some years before his death. He seems also to have had shares in two vessels called the *Lily* and the *Swallow*, which must have been registered in Liverpool. The gross value of his estate in England was assessed at £1,234.11s., including, presumably, some liquid financial assets. In the Isle of Man there was still 'my cottage garden and paddock', a small part of the Rose Hill estate which had been retained when the rest was sold in 1875.

Mary was named joint executor of Thomas's will with a John Fallows of Liverpool. Fallows must have been an agent or close associate of the family, for he is also named in the report of the wreck of the *Serica* which is held in the National Maritime Museum. There is a reference there to correspondence from a John Fallows of Princes Park, 20 Bentley Road, Liverpool, who had received news in June 1868 – while Thomas and Mary were still en route home from Mauritius – that 'the master is expected home early in September'. This presumably means that news of the loss of the ship, and the deaths of Tom and James, reached the Isle of Man and their other children before they did.

Mary Cubbin and John Fallows appear to have dealt with the English part of Thomas's estate, but then demurred at the Manx part. At a special ecclesiastical court held on 30th September 1882 a Thomas Kneen of Douglas was approved as 'advocate administrator' of the will. In essence, Thomas had directed that all his assets be realised, and the income held in trust 'for my dear wife … and such of my daughters Mary, Jane, Amy and Serica Isabella as shall live to attain the age of twenty-one years'. He was even careful to direct that each daughter should enjoy their income 'free from the debts control or engagements of any husband to whom she may be married'. Only Esther was not mentioned, presumably because she was already married when the will was made, and Thomas was quite satisfied that she would be comfortably provided for by the Cubbon family.

When she sought probate for Thomas's will, Mary's address was given as 19 Brisbane Street, Douglas, but she clearly soon returned to China. In due course Jane, Amy and Serica all found husbands amongst the expatriate community there. Jane became Mrs Conner (the mother of Thomas Conner, who had been born in China but was with his aunt Esther in Douglas in 1901), and young Mary become Mrs Hurst, although it is not known where or when these marriages took place. Then on 4th December 1886 the following death notice appeared in the *Isle of Man Examiner*:

> October 3rd, at Shanghai, China, Mary widow of Capt. Thos. Cubbin, late of Rose Hill, Braddan.

Mary's two remaining daughters were both married in the British Consulate at Tientsin the following year: Amy became the wife of thirty-five year old Alexander Robertson on 25th July 1887, and Serica was married to Hector John Macrae, who was twenty-eight, on 10th October. The professions of both men were given as 'engineer'. Serica, the child who must have been such a consolation to her parents when she was born in 1870, is said to have been interned in a Japanese prisoner of war camp during World War Two, but there is a record of a Serica I. Grimshaw arriving in New York in 1946. Hector Macrae died in 1902, and Grimshaw is believed to have been the name of her second husband.

Thomas and Mary's grandson John enjoyed a Customs career in China which lasted from 1905 into the late 1930s, and a great-grandson, James, was born in Nanking. During World War II this branch of the family moved, initially back to England, and later to California, where our informant, James Cubbon II, was born in 1954.

There is a sad postscript to the story of Charles Radcliffe, the fourteen-year-old ship's boy from the *Serica* whom the Cubbins had to leave in hospital on St Helena on their way home. Somehow he made his way back to Liverpool when he had recovered his strength, but he never went to sea again. The son of a shipwright, when in 1875 he married Clara Lawson, a shipwright's daughter, at St Bride's Church in Liverpool, he was described as an office clerk. But by January 1885 he was dead of pulmonary tuberculosis. The same disease carried twenty-nine-year-old Clara off just ten months later. They left three orphaned children to be brought up by relatives.

As for the next generation of Thomas and Mary Cubbin's family – when their daughter Esther Cubbon gave birth to her own youngest daughter in 1896, she named the child Ethel Serica. They simply could never forget.

Publication

Thomas Cubbin's memoir *The Wreck of the Serica: The Wonderful Adventures of a Manxman* was published simultaneously in 1870 by Mylrea & Allen in Douglas, Edward Howell in Liverpool, and Simpkins, Marshall & Co. in London. It sold for five shillings, but it is not known how many copies were printed. Even if it was only a few hundred, it must have attracted considerable attention, and not only in Britain. It was even on the reading list for 1870-1 of the American psychologist and philosopher William James. According to Robert D. Richardson in his book *William James: In the Maelstrom of American Modernism*, James 'read Alfred Russel Wallace's *Malay Archipelago*, Raphael Pumpelly's *Across America and Asia*, and the travel writing of Georg Forster, who had been around the world with Captain Thomas Cook. He read Henry Thoreau's *A Week on the Concord and Merrimack Rivers*, Thomas Cubbin's *Wreck of the Serica*, Jane Smith's *Captivity Amongst Indians*, and Daniel Drake's *Pioneer Life in Kentucky*'.

The Manx National Heritage Library's copy arrived in the Isle of Man in 1923, having been part of the collection of Streatham-based George William Wood. There are two inscriptions in it relating to the Cubbins, unfortunately both inaccurate. On the flyleaf Wood had written, 'Mr Cubbin and his wife went to live at Rose Hill, Braddan, Isle of Man, on his retirement from the sea. It is not recorded whether he died there or went abroad and died'. Even more misleadingly, on the endpaper he copied out the *Isle of Man Examiner*'s 1886 death notice for Mary Cubbin, but mistakenly transcribed 'wife of' rather than 'widow of Capt. Thos. Cubbin of Rose Hill', as the *Examiner* correctly had it.

In his *Bibliography of the Literature of the Isle of Man* William Cubbon says of *The Wreck of the Serica*, 'Only one copy of this book is known'. He must be referring to the one in the Manx Museum, because he also quotes Wood's inaccurate inscription about Cubbin's 'retirement' to Rose Hill. But there are other copies of this original edition in private hands; local auctioneer Murray Keefe offered one at a sale in May 2007.

A copy also came up in Christie's King Street saleroom in London in 2004, when a lot which also included two other, probably much more valuable, books went for £956. All came from the collection of the eccentric adventurer and explorer Quentin Keynes, who had died the previous year. Tantalizingly, the sale list recorded that it was 'a presentation copy from Mary Cubbins and with a signed inscription by the author on the rear endpaper recto'. It is believed to have passed through the hands of the London dealers Maggs Bros. Rare Books, who bought it from Christie's, to a New York collector of shipwreck stories.

In 1950 the Dropmore Press of London published a reprint, limited to three hundred numbered copies, with handsome if rather inaccurate wood engravings by John Worsley, and an introduction by the maritime author H. M. Tomlinson. Dropmore appear to have decided to play down Cubbin's Manx identity, as their dust jacket describes him as 'Master Mariner of Liverpool'. A small number of copies of this edition can usually be found offered for sale on the internet.

An odd spin-off from the 1950 reprint was an excitable lecture given by Dr Eugene Vest, professor of English at the University of Illinois, in a radio series entitled 'This Great Wide World', delivered between 1949-1952. There is nothing in this lecture which was not in the original account, but the author has a recording of it which in due course will be lodged in the Manx National Heritage Library.

A selection of the more dramatic parts of the story was also republished in 2004, in *The Mammoth Book of Shipwrecks and Sea Disasters*, which was compiled and edited by Richard Russell Lawrence.

APPENDIX II

Thomas Cubbin's service record

In the course of his career Thomas Cubbin served on the following vessels. Details of the first seven are from his application for a Master's Certificate (National Maritime Museum, cert. no. 2721), and the remainder from his service record as a merchant naval officer (National Archives, BT 122/59). Further information about individual vessels has already been given in the Foreword and Afterword.

Mona (ON 3879, built in the Isle of Man, 1833), reg. Liverpool.

Mary Elizabeth, reg. Liverpool.

Landford, reg. Liverpool.

Sherbrooke, reg. Cork.

Majestic (ON 25888), reg. Liverpool.

Indus (ON 25789), reg. Liverpool.

Wilson, reg. Liverpool.

Rock City (ON 15900), reg. Liverpool.

Caribou (ON 1400), reg. Liverpool.

Ocean Gem (ON 25744), reg. Liverpool.

Wild Dayrell (ON 47588), reg. Liverpool.

Helvetia (ON 51401), reg. Liverpool.

Serica (ON 48780, formerly the *Estelle*), reg. Liverpool.

Ocean Gem (ON 47281), reg. Douglas, Isle of Man.

Cassowary (ON 64708), reg. Douglas, Isle of Man.

*Mary (*ON 50263), originally *Alexandra* (reg. Liverpool), then *Mary* (reg. Liverpool), then *S.G.G. Thompson* (reg. Plymouth). Thomas Cubbin reverted to the name *Mary*; the vessel's final registration was in Shanghai.

*Official Numbers (ON) were issued to all British seagoing vessels extant
in 1855 in order to give each ship a unique identity. Official numbers for the*
Mary Elizabeth, Landford, Sherbrooke *and* Wilson *have not been found.*

Crew agreement for the Serica's 1867-8 voyage (inscriptions on the left are against the names of those who did not return). There is no indication that Mary and her sons were on board.

APPENDIX III

Abandon Ship!

When the *Serica* was abandoned, the Cubbins and their crew transferred into the vessel's two small boats. Thomas divided them into two groups of nine:

FIRST BOAT

Thomas Cubbin, Master, aged 45
Mary Ann Cubbin, 39
Thomas Cubbin jnr., 11★★
James Cubbin, 22 months★★
John Cruickshank, Chief Mate, 22
Andrew Stout, 28
Thomas Hall, 42★★
William Edward Clarke, 17
Charles Alexander Radcliffe, 14

★ Died before landing on Madagascar.
★★ Died during landing at Mahila Bay.

SECOND BOAT

David Nicholson, 2nd Mate, 28
Daniel Roberts, 39★★★
Alexander MacKenzie, 28★
Alexander McKenzie, 40
Edward Fennell, 25
Edward Kiffin (Giffen), 22★★★
Jeremiah Driscoll, 42★★★★
Antonio Jenkins, 42
Joseph Mar——, 36

★★★ Died at Tamatave.
★★★★ Died on passage home from Mauritius.

Thomas and Jane Cubbin

Others inc. child died 1813, Thomas, b. 1809, d.
1821, and William, b.1827, d.1864 in Shanghai

THOMAS CUBBIN m. MARY ANN WAGSTAFF

27.10.1847, St Mark's Church, Upper Duke Street, Liverpool

b. Derbyhaven (Castletown),
Isle of Man, 20.2.1823,
d. Chefoo, China, 3.11.1881.

b. Liverpool 1827,
d. Shanghai,
China, 3.10.1886.

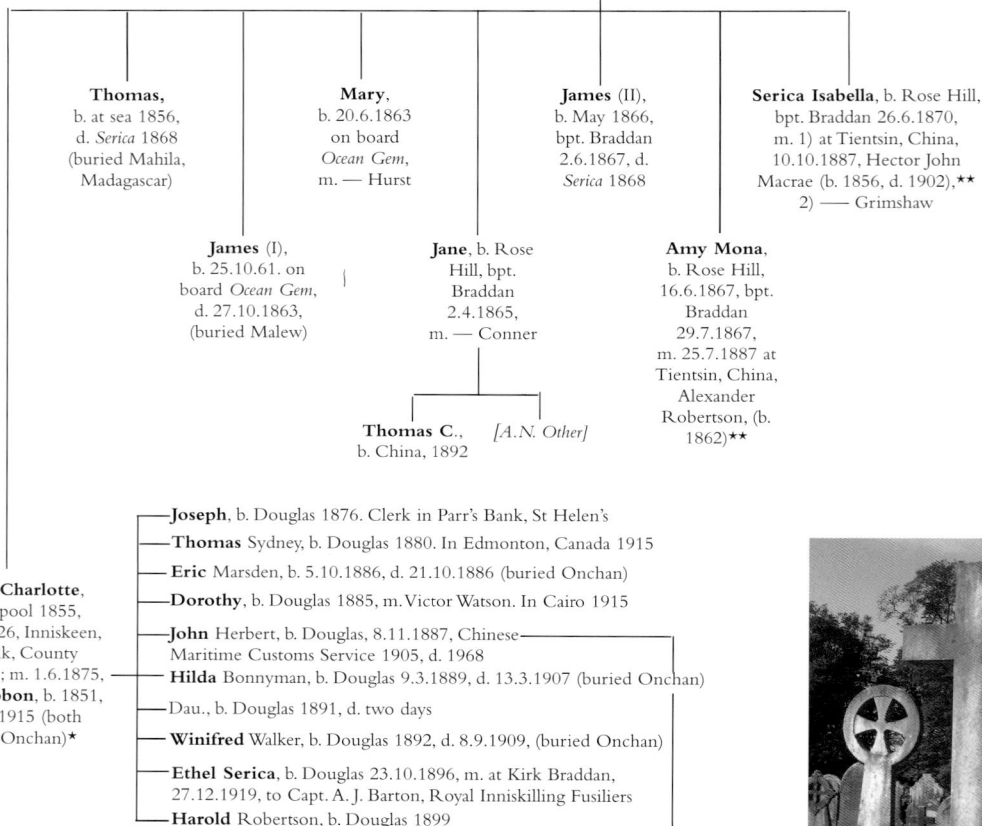

Thomas,
b. at sea 1856,
d. *Serica* 1868
(buried Mahila,
Madagascar)

Mary,
b. 20.6.1863
on board
Ocean Gem,
m. — Hurst

James (II),
b. May 1866,
bpt. Braddan
2.6.1867, d.
Serica 1868

Serica Isabella, b. Rose Hill,
bpt. Braddan 26.6.1870,
m. 1) at Tientsin, China,
10.10.1887, Hector John
Macrae (b. 1856, d. 1902),★★
2) — Grimshaw

James (I),
b. 25.10.61. on
board *Ocean Gem*,
d. 27.10.1863,
(buried Malew)

Jane, b. Rose
Hill, bpt.
Braddan
2.4.1865,
m. — Conner

Amy Mona,
b. Rose Hill,
16.6.1867, bpt.
Braddan
29.7.1867,
m. 25.7.1887 at
Tientsin, China,
Alexander
Robertson, (b.
1862)★★

Thomas C.,
b. China, 1892

[A.N. Other]

Joseph, b. Douglas 1876. Clerk in Parr's Bank, St Helen's

Thomas Sydney, b. Douglas 1880. In Edmonton, Canada 1915

Eric Marsden, b. 5.10.1886, d. 21.10.1886 (buried Onchan)

Dorothy, b. Douglas 1885, m. Victor Watson. In Cairo 1915

John Herbert, b. Douglas, 8.11.1887, Chinese
Maritime Customs Service 1905, d. 1968

Hilda Bonnyman, b. Douglas 9.3.1889, d. 13.3.1907 (buried Onchan)

Dau., b. Douglas 1891, d. two days

Winifred Walker, b. Douglas 1892, d. 8.9.1909, (buried Onchan)

Ethel Serica, b. Douglas 23.10.1896, m. at Kirk Braddan,
27.12.1919, to Capt. A. J. Barton, Royal Inniskilling Fusiliers

Harold Robertson, b. Douglas 1899

Esther Charlotte,
b. Liverpool 1855,
d. 12.2.1926, Inniskeen,
Dundalk, County
Monaghan; m. 1.6.1875,
John Cubbon, b. 1851,
d. 18.7.1915 (both
buried Onchan)★

James,
b. China 1925

James (II),
b. USA 1954

★ At the time of the 1881 Census, John and Esther Cubbon were living at 8 Albert
Terrace, Douglas, Isle of Man; in 1891 ditto with three servants; in 1901, in Alexander
Drive with two servants; in 1911 at Holmlea, Albany Road, with two servants.

★★ Both couples were living in Taku at the time they were married.

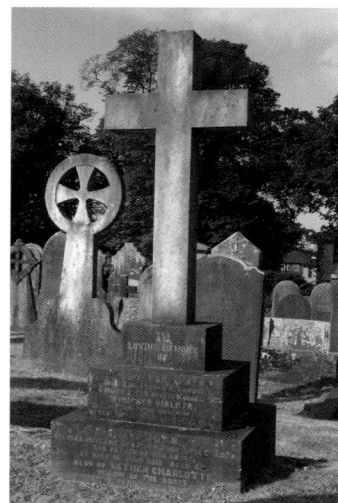

CUBBIN FAMILY TREE

PHOTO BY VALERIE COTTLE

The grave at Kirk Onchan of John and
Esther Cubbon, buried with their
children Eric, Hilda and Winifred.

NOTES

Thomas Cubbin was born in the hamlet of Derbyhaven... Thomas's merchant naval records always name Castletown as his birthplace, but this would be quite usual for somebody born in the nearby small fishing hamlet; his birth in Derbyhaven is confirmed by his great-great-grandson James Cubbon, and also by Marion Bolam, who was married to a descendant of one of his brothers. It has not been possible to find a record of his birth or baptism amongst Manx archives; his birthdate is taken from the Register of Seamen's Tickets (1845-54) at National Archives (NA), BT 113/8. The name and occupation of Thomas Cubbin snr are from Thomas's marriage certificate (Liverpool, 1847). A gravestone in Malew churchyard seems to indicate that Thomas's parents were named Thomas and Jane, and that siblings included an older Thomas who died in 1821, after whom our Thomas was named.

Page 11

Dorothy Wordsworth, passing through... Dorothy Wordsworth, Journal of *a Tour in the Isle of Man*, 1828.

Page 13

Castletown's population of just over two thousand... *Pigot's Directory*, 1824.

In the Isle of Man the hero of the Battle of Trafalgar... John Quilliam (1771-1829) is buried in Arbory Churchyard, where a commemoration of his life still takes place every year on Trafalgar Day.

Kept a fishing smack of his own... Derek Winterbottom, *Profile of Castletown*, 2010, p.91.

Married a local heiress... Margaret Christian Stevenson was a younger daughter of Richard Ambrose Stevenson of Balladoole, and was the heiress of Ballakaighen (the spelling varies), another Stevenson property nearby.

In 1822 a National School had been opened... 'Minute Book of the Castletown National School 1820-1850', Manx National Heritage Library (MNHL) MS5668C.

Page 14

Taubman's Endowed School... 'Taubman's School is for teaching... navigation', *Pigot's Directory* 1837.

He was described as being five foot seven-and-a-half inches tall... The description of Thomas Cubbin's physique is taken from the Register of Seamen's Tickets as above (NA) BT 113/8.

Becoming an AB... The first rank on the deck of a merchant ship was that of the unlicensed Ordinary Seaman. The AB (Able Seaman) had taken a more advanced training, and was able to assume greater responsibilities.

Page 15

The case of apprentice Daniel Dickinson... *Cumberland Pacquet and Ware's Whitehaven Advertiser*, 17th October 1865. Quoted at *www.mightyseas.co.uk/marhist/whitehaven/ehen.htm*

An apprentice had to learn the name... Susanne Störmer, *William McMaster Murdoch: A Career at Sea*, Stormbreakers Verlag E. K, 2002.

Page 16

The first steamship had crossed the Atlantic... The SS *Savannah*, an American-built sailing ship with a steam-powered sidewheel, is generally accepted to have been the first steamship to cross the Atlantic. However not much of her 1819 journey was actually accomplished under steam.

Page 17

A small steamer was making the weekly return trip... The *Triton* was plying the Douglas-Whitehaven route by 1826. The Isle of Man Steam Packet Company, which is still in service, was founded in 1830 (initially calling itself the Mona's Isle Company), Derek Winterbottom, 'Economic History, 1830-1996', in *A New History of the Isle of Man*, Vol. 5 2000, p.217-18.

This great, turbulent, monstrous port... Most of the statistics in the folllowing passage are taken from Graeme J. Milne, 'Maritime Liverpool', in *Liverpool 800: Culture, Character & History*, ed. John Belchem, 2006.

Linked by trade to 'every port of any importance in every quarter of the globe'... T. Baines, *History of the Commerce and Town of Liverpool*, 1852, p.840, quoted by Graeme J. Milne, ibid.

The most vivid account of dock life... Herman Melville's *Redburn: His First Voyage, Being the Sailor Boy Confessions and Reminiscences of The Son-Of-A-Gentleman In the Merchant Navy*, is a fictionalized account, published ten years after the event, of the American author's voyage to Liverpool in 1839.

Page 19

Notorious Corinthian haunts... St Paul, in his first letter to the church he had founded in Corinth, lamented the sexual immorality of the city, 'First Epistle of Paul the Apostle to the Corinthians', esp. Chapter V.

Page 20

Campeachy Campeche, on the Mexican Yucatan peninsula, gave its name (corrupted to 'Campeachy') to the timber the area produced.

Page 22

From Liverpool to Batavia... the name given by the Dutch East India Company to the ancient port of Jayakarta in Java, during their colonisation of the region from the early seventeenth century on. It reverted to being called Jakarta in 1942, and was made capital of Indonesia after World War II. Details of Thomas Cubbin's early voyages are attached to his application for a Master's Certificate (National Maritime Museum, cert. no. 2721).

A newspaper report for October 1844... *Shipping Gazette and Sydney General Trade List*, Vol. 1, No. 30, 12th October 1844.

Headed for Bombay... the city's name has officially been Mumbai for English-speakers since 1995.

Page 23 **Mate on the *Sherbrooke*...** No trace of this vessel has been found in Lloyd's List, but the previous year the *Montreal Transport* reported, 'Arrived at the Port of Quebec 20th May 1846 – Ship *Sherbrooke* from Cork (sailed 15th April)'. *www.theshipslist.com*

Twenty-year-old Mary Ann Wagstaff... Although the 1871 Isle of Man census states that Mary Ann Cubbin was born in 1829, her marriage certificate in 1847 gives her age as twenty, i.e. she was born in 1827. This is more likely to be right – nineteenth century censuses are frequently inaccurate as far as ages and birth dates are concerned.

St Mark's Church... was built in 1803, officially consecrated in 1815, but abandoned and demolished in 1913 (*www.old-liverpool.co.uk/church-closures.html*) when its congregation decamped to the new Anglican Cathedral, built on St James' Mount to the south of Upper Hope Street. It is described in *A Picture of Liverpool: The Stranger's Guide*, 1834, as being built of brick with a square tower. It offered seating for 1,714 people and 'a handsome organ'.

On this side of the Atlantic at least... The lives of the wives of nineteenth-century American mariners are given masterly coverage in Joan Druett, *Hen Frigates: Wives of Merchant Captains Under Sail*, 1998. She draws on a rich treasury of unpublished letters and diaries, but hardly any of her material is taken from the British side of the Atlantic.

Page 25 **The House of Commons Select Committee...** Maranham is indicated as one of 'the places where slavers land their cargoes and also where they are fitted out for slave trading', on a map commissioned by the Committee and published by J. Arrowsmith of London on 22nd July 1850, *www.memory.loc.gov/ammem/index.html*

A record-breaking run... In the *Daily Southern Cross* (see *www.freepages.genealogy.rootsweb. ancestry.com*) Further details of the voyage are in Henry Brett's *White Winds*, Vol. II, 1928, online at *www.nzetc.org* Brett says that the vessel carried seventeen passengers on her record-breaking run, as opposed to the *Daily Southern Cross* report of nineteen, and has her sailing from Gravesend on 6th March rather than the 4th. The fact remains that the voyage was a remarkable achievement.

Page 26 **'Capt. Cubbins [*sic*]...'** Throughout his career, in every context outside the Isle of Man where the surname Cubbin or Cubbon is common, Thomas was referred to both officially and unofficially as 'Cubbins'. He made Mary Ann Wagstaff 'Mrs Cubbins' in Liverpool in 1847, and this led to what one hopes was some good-natured contention later in their lives. When they bought a house in the Isle of Man in 1863, Thomas signed the indentures with the familiar Manx version 'Thomas Cubbin'; Mary signed as 'Mary Cubbins'. He often seems to have avoided the issue by adding a downward flourish, not exactly an 's', to the end of his signature. When Mary applied for administration of his estate in the Isle of Man in 1882, she signed her name firmly 'Cubbins'. Another – presumably Manx – hand has equally firmly scored the final 's' out on the Manx Museum's copy of the will (Thomas Cubbin Last Will & Testament, MNHL 166).

One regrettable duty to attend to... Inquest on James Bruce, reported by the *Daily Southern Cross*, 26 June 1855, p.5.

Page 27 **On this occasion Thomas was to make a surprising discovery...** The *Colonist* newspaper, founded at Nelson on the South Island of New Zealand in 1857, reported on 14th September 1858 (issue 94, p.4) under the heading Curious Discovery in the South Atlantic, copying a letter written by Captain Cubins [*sic*] of the *Caribou* to the Secretary of the Admiralty in London. Dated Ship *Caribou*, Hobson's Bay [Auckland, at that time New Zealand's capital city], March 13, 1858. *www.paperspast.natlib.govt.nz/cgi-bin/paperspast* and *www.heardisland.aq* Heard Island and the McDonald Islands (HIMI) have been Australian territory since 1947, and are now administered by the Antarctic Division of Australia's Department of the Environment and Heritage.

Page 30 **Mary Cubbin gave birth to a son...** With reference to the location of this birth, so far south when the *Ocean Gem* was en route for China, Alistair Roach (pers. comm.) refers to a contemporary map, 'Sailing Ship Routes to and from Far Eastern Ports'. He explains, 'Prior to the Suez Canal being built it appears that the preferred route to China, once clear of the Cape of Good Hope, was to head north-eastwards and up towards Java and Borneo, thus taking advantage of the prevailing winds and currents between the months of October and March. At other times of the year ships favoured the Great Eastern Route. This took them south of Australia and Tasmania, then northwards between Australia and New Zealand and onwards towards the Solomon Islands. The route then splits, one part going to Hong Kong and the other to Yokohama in Japan. If Cubbin didn't want to wend his way through Indonesia, if the winds or currents were wrong, he would have stuck to this route'.

Reopened as a Treaty Port... The first British Treaty Ports were established in China by the Treaty of Nanking *Page 31* in 1842, at the end of the First Opium War. They were at Ningpo (which translates into the welcoming 'serene waves'), Shanghai, Canton, Fuchow, and Amoy. A second group of Treaty Ports was set up following the end of the Arrow War in 1860. Under the so-called Unequal Treaties, foreigners were allowed to settle and trade on the edges of existing port cities, while enjoying extra-territorial legal rights.

£1,150 on a 'mansion'... Rose Hill was bought 'by T. Cubbon [sic] of Castletown' from Thomas and Mary *Page 32* Kneale, and the Cubbins paid an additional £665 to Edward Caryl Fleetwood and his wife Elizabeth for part of the Booilrenny (modern Bulrhenny) farmland. The conveyances are in the Manx National Heritage Library (Book 4156, p.347 and Book 4202, p.351 respectively). A total of £1,815 in 1863 represents something over £1 milllion today, as related to average earnings (*www.measuringworth.com*). Thomas's flagstaff is clearly marked on the 1866 Ordnance Survey map of the area. The house still stands, but a number of modern extensions have been added since 1990.

Nassau ... quickly became one of the main hubs... James Russell Soley, 'The Blockading of the Southern *Page 34* Seaports in the Civil War' in *The Blockade and the Cruisers*, 1885 at *www.civilwarhome. com/blockade.htm*

'Does anyone who knows Liverpool...' *Liverpool Albion*, May 1862, quoted by Norman Longmate, *The Hungry* *Page 35* *Mills*, 1978, p.253-4, and again at *www.americancivilwar.org.uk*

'That nest of pirates'... 'Mr. Barclay, former [British] consul at New York... called on me with reference to cotton claimed by English subjects. He seemed amazed when I told him ... that in no event would I treat an English subject with more favor than one of our own deluded citizens, and that for my part I was unwilling to fight for cotton for the benefit of Englishmen openly engaged in smuggling arms and instruments of war to kill us; that, on the contrary, it would afford me great satisfaction to conduct my army to Nassau, and wipe out that nest of pirates'. Major General William T. Sherman to Edwin Stanton, Secretary of War, January 1865 (*www.americancivilwar.org.uk*)

His job was simply to deliver the *Wild Dayrell*... The blockade runner *Wild Dayrell* was built by Jones, Quiggin & Co., founded in 1855, which became the Liverpool Shipbuilding Co. Ltd in 1865. They built everything from paddle steamers for Indian rivers to barges used on the Nile, ocean-going iron sailing ships to a steam gondola for Coniston Water. One of their five blockade runners, the *Banshee*, was the first steel ship to cross the Atlantic in 1863.

On her final voyage, in early February... Details of the *Wild Dayrell*'s cargo from Raymond Tubby, unpublished master's thesis, University of East Carolina, 2000, p.173, accessed via *www.saw.usace.army.mil*

Tom would have been familiar... The first half of the nineteenth century had seen the founding of some forty publications like *The Youth's Magazine, or Evangelical Miscellany* (founded in 1805), *The Children's Friend* (1824), and *The Child's Companion, or, Sunday Scholar's Reward* (1824-1932).

The emigrant steamer *Helvetia*... Crew list as per log/crew agreement, held by the University of Newfoundland; *Page 36* passenger list as per the Immigrant Ships Transcribers' Guild, accessed at *www.immigrantships.net/v9/1800v9/helvetia 118670218.html* The diary account is by Robert Nicholson Tate (1804-86), of his return voyage as a cabin passenger leaving Liverpool for New York on 23rd October 1867, accessed at *www.theshipslist.com/accounts/tate.htm*

Coal is notoriously dangerous... 'Lady Brassey, an Englishwoman who sailed about the world on her husband's *Page 38* luxury yacht in 1876, wrote after recording an encounter with a bark on fire that out of every three ships that carried coal or coke, one caught fire on the way round the Horn'. *Around the World on the Yacht "Sunbeam": Our Home on the Ocean for Eleven Months*, New York, 1878, quoted in Joan Druett, *Hen Frigates*.

The death of Captain Archibald Lister... *Cumberland Pacquet and Ware's Whitehaven Advertiser*, 30th March 1860.

The 783-ton *Volunteer*... *Liverpool Mercury*, 4th February 1864. Following details via *www.mightyseas.co.uk*

Page 41   **Akyab in Burma...** Now Sitwe.

Tessa Karran ... would recall... From 'The Children of the Manx King' by Tessa Kinvig (*née* Karran), MNHL MS10884/2. In the same MS, written late in her life, she describes an idyllic memory: 'Even now it is so vivid to me, the warm comfortable cabin, Mother reading to us, Constance [the children's governess] making hot cocoa, the tramp, tramp of the sailors overhead, the creaking of the ship and the noise of the waves splashing over [her], and my father and Captain Pratt [his second in command] coming into the cabin in gleaming wet oilskins with axes tied round their waists ready to cut away masts or gear that had broken loose, and both of them making jokes and laughing with us when there was an extra loud crash. Then, being left to amuse ourselves for the rest of the night, saying our prayers and going to sleep to the sound of my mother's beautiful voice singing our favourite song, "White wings that never grow weary" – white wings, of course, being the sails of the ship'.

Page 42   **In *The Nigger of the Narcissus*...** The sea stories of Joseph Conrad (1857-1924) are more evocative than any other writing of life in the mercantile marine at this time, and especially as far as sailors in the Indian Ocean and Far East are concerned.

The *Serica*'s crew... In his introduction to the Dropmore Press edition of *The Wreck of the Serica,* published in London in 1950, Henry Major Tomlinson remarks that: 'In those days life at sea did not invariably attract the best of men... the *Serica* appears to have collected a miserable bunch of poltroons'.

Page 43   **Twenty-two year old Edward Kiffin...** This surname is given as 'Giffen' in some documents relating to the *Serica*, but Kiffin accords with his birth certificate. The full crew list is taken from the log/crew agreement for the voyage, which is held in the Maritime History Archive of the Memorial University of Newfoundland.

Page 45   **The chief port of Tamatave...** Modern Toamasina, still the island's main port. Thanks to modern technology, anyone with access to Google Earth can type in 'Mahela, Madagascar', and follow the Cubbins' route all the way up the coast to Toamasina; it is in fact the best way of appreciating the nature of the terrain. The main change since their day is that in the 1890s French engineers linked all the inland coastal waterways together, so that most of the way could be travelled by boat. There is now a coastal road, but travel in Madagascar is still not for the faint-hearted.

Page 46   **The Bishop of Mauritius wrote...** Vincent W. Ryan, D.D., Bishop of Mauritius, *Journals of An Eight Years' Residence in the Diocese of Mauritius, and of a Visit to Madagascar*, 1864, at *www.anglicanhistory.org*

The Austrian traveller Ida Pfeiffer... Ida Pfeiffer, *The Last Travels of Ida Pfeiffer, inclusive of a Visit to Madagascar*, 1861, p.137, at *www.onread.com/reader/1354710*

Page 48   **Ranavalona I was one of the great monsters...** For a full account of Ranavalona's reign, see Keith Laidler's *Female Caligula: Ranavalona, the Mad Queen of Madagascar*, 2005. The queen featured in fictional form in George MacDonald Fraser's *Flashman's Lady*, 1977.

The missionary William Ellis... William Ellis of the London Missionary Society, *Madagascar Revisited*, 1867, at *www.readingbook.com* Contemporary accounts of Madagascar include Lyons McLeod's *Madagascar and its People*, 1865.

Page 50   **Another member of the London Missionary Society...** Ebenezer Prout, *Madagascar, its Mission and its Martyrs*, 1863. The LMS started to send missionaries to Madagascar in 1862, once the persecution of Christians under Queen Ranavalona I came to an end.

THE WRECK OF THE SERICA

Page 51   **To cry to the sea...** The quotation used on the title page of the 1870 edition of *The Wreck of the Serica* is taken from *The Tempest* (Act I, Scene 2), where Prospero is trying to console his daughter Miranda after they have been shipwrecked. It is not known whether this was Thomas Cubbin's choice, or the publisher's.

Page 64   **If Miss Burdett Coutts had been there...** Angela Burdett-Coutts (1814-1906) inherited a £3 million fortune in 1837, and became perhaps the greatest public philanthropist of her time. Her numerous 'causes' included a close involvement with the Royal Society for the Prevention of Cruelty to Animals. She was made a baroness in her own right by Queen Victoria in 1871.

The traveller's tree... The Traveller's Tree or Traveller's Palm, *Ravenala madagascariensis*, is not a true palm, but related to the genus Strelitzia. A large fan-shaped tree, it has leaf stems which catch and hold rainwater and dew, so has long been used by travellers as an emergency water supply.   *Page 75*

Our very kind friend Mr Liger... It has not proved possible to trace any of the people who helped Thomas and Mary Cubbin in Madagascar, apart from the Revds Thomas Campbell and Herbert Maundrell, who are known to have been the first missionaries sent out to the island in 1862 by the Church Missionary Society.   *Page 78*

Hova or government officer... The Hovas were a caste of the ruling Merina dynasty, probably of Malay descent, and held most public positions at this time.   *Page 85*

Consul Pakenham would pay... H.B.M. Consul in Madagascar in 1868 was a T. C. Pakenham.   *Page 91*

Must have their kabara... The *kabara* seems to have been a semi-formal discussion, without which a group could not proceed to any action. Thomas saw it largely as a time-wasting exercise on the part of his attendants.

More commonly called a bullocker... 'The chief exports from Madagascar are horned cattle for the markets of Mauritius and Réunion. More than 10,000 are annually shipped for the former place', *Madagascar Revisited*, William Ellis, London Missionary Society, 1867, p.19. Most cattle in Madagascar are still of the long-horned zebu type.   *Page 104*

We had two Limas... Thomas probably never saw this word written down, and had never seen lemurs before.   *Page 106*

AFTERWORD

Its ferocity was reported around the world... Newspaper reports from *www.paperspast.natlib.govt.nz* Sir Henry Barkly (1815-98) was in turn Governor of British Guiana, Jamaica, Victoria, and, from 1863-70, of Mauritius.   *Page 116*

Two days before the estate was sold... MNHL Requisition Book 4508, page 347, deed no. 82; Requisition Book 1773, page 137, deed no. 61.   *Page 117*

He had led his eldest daughter... Esther's marriage to John Cubbon would have taken place in 'Old' Kirk Braddan, like the baptisms of all the younger Cubbin children. The present Kirk Braddan church was not opened until the following year.   *Page 118*

When John Cubbon died suddenly in 1915... Obituary, *Isle of Man Examiner*, 24th July 1915.

Living in Liverpool... The River Avon Street address appears on Thomas's service record (NA) BT 122/59.   *Page 120*

During the American Civil War... Merseyside Maritime Museum Information Sheet No. 59, 'Liverpool and the American Civil War' at *www.liverpoolmuseums.org.uk/maritime*

A Confederate naval officer... The following information about the *Alexandra/Mary*'s record during the Civil War period is from Richard I. Lester, 'The Procurement of Confederate Blockade Runners and other vessels in Great Britain during the American Civil War', *The Mariner's Mirror*, Vol. 61, No. 3, 1975.

There is a note at the end... Thomas's service record as above (NA) BT 122/59.   *Page 121*

The notorious Black Book... A record of disciplinary measures taken against officers found to have acted recklessly in their handling of vessels at sea. Copies are held both by National Archives and the National Maritime Museum, Greenwich.

A letter dated 18th December 1904... *The I.G. in Peking*, vol II, ed. John King Fairbank, Harvard, 1975.

It was even on the reading list... Robert D. Richardson, *William James: In the Maelstrom of American Modernism*, 2006, p.125.   *Page 126*

In his *Bibliography*... William Cubbon, *Bibliography of the Literature of the Isle of Man*, Vol. I, 1933, p.87.

An odd spin-off... In the Eugene B. Vest Tape Collection, University of Illinois at Chicago Library, 011-08-21-01, Box 2, Folder 47.   *Page 127*

ON BOARD THE ss *GREAT BRITAIN*, BRISTOL DOCKS.

VALERIE COTTLE has a BA in English from Bristol University, and has spent most of her working life as a journalist and editor of newspapers, magazines and books published in the Isle of Man.

ALISTAIR ROACH holds an MPhil in Maritime History and Archaeology and is an Associate of the Institute for Archaeology. Having retired from the National Trust he now assists at The Brunel Institute (ss *Great Britain* Trust) and is a freelance maritime artist and researcher.